S0-APN-190

 DESKTOP PUBLISHER'S SURVIVAL KIT

DESKTOP PUBLISHER'S SURVIVAL KIT

DAVID BLATNER

AN OPEN
HOUSE BOOK

PEACHPIT
PRESS

క్ర

To Alisa Joy Blatner, my sister and my friend

DESKTOP PUBLISHER'S SURVIVAL KIT
David Blatner

PEACHPIT PRESS, INC.
2414 Sixth Street
Berkeley, CA 94710
(510) 548-4393
(510) 548-5991 (fax)

Copyright © 1991 by David Blatner
Cover design by Studio Silicon
Interior design by Olav Martin Kvern

All rights reserved. No part of this book may be reproduced or transmitted in any form or by any means, electronic, mechanical, photocopying, recording, or otherwise, without the prior written permission of the publisher. For information, contact Peachpit Press.

PERMISSIONS:
Page 79, Figure 7-2 reprinted with permission of Special Collections Division, University of Washington Libraries (photo by Cobb, negative no. 10509). Page 82, Figure 7-5 reprinted with permission of Special Collections Division, University of Washington Libraries (photo by Todd, negative no. 10511).

NOTICE OF LIABILITY:
The information in this book is distributed on an "As is" basis, without warranty. While every precaution has been taken in the preparation of this book, neither the author nor Peachpit Press, Inc., shall have any liability to any person or entity with respect to any liability, loss, or damage caused or alleged to be caused directly or indirectly by the instructions contained in this book or by the computer software and hardware products described herein.

TRADEMARKS:
Throughout this book, trademarked names are used. Rather than put a trademark symbol in every occurrence of a trademarked name, we are using the names only in an editorial fashion and to the benefit of the trademark owner, with no intention of infringement of the trademark. Where those designations appear in this book, the designations have been printed in initial caps.

ISBN 0-938151-76-2

0 9 8 7 6 5 4 3 2 1

Printed and bound in the United States of America

OVERVIEW

CONTENTS

CHAPTER 1

THE JUNGLES

I don't know about you, but my mother never warned me about the *real* jungles. Oh, she warned me about the wild ways of the world, the dangerous-looking people with yellow neckties, and even the struggle to be real in this world of prefabricated lunch meat. But she never told me about the worst of it. She never told me about desktop publishing.

I guess she can't be blamed, though. Desktop publishing came on like a storm, surprising everyone (even the folks who made it happen, like Apple Computer and Aldus Corporation). In a matter of just a few years, hundreds of thousands of people have started to use the computer as a graphic arts tool. Some of them were artists who had never used a computer before in their lives. Others had a more technical background, and jumped at the opportunity to "get artsy" in a brave new world.

THE GURUS

Out of this mish-mash of newly self-proclaimed "desktop publishers" came a select few who always seemed to know the answers to questions like "Why aren't these files working?" and "How can I get this picture to look right?" These are the gurus.

Gurus come in all shapes and sizes. The ones with technical backgrounds are often called "bit-heads," "techno-weenies," or "tweaks." The ones with design backgrounds are often called "production artists" or "Macintosh specialists." But whatever they're called, one thing is for certain. They have somehow come upon The Knowledge, which has raised them to their current status.

I don't mean to sound like a bad television evangelist, but believe me when I tell you that it's easier to gain The Knowledge and become a guru than you think. Sure, it takes perseverance. Sure, it takes hard work. But you've taken the first step by picking up this book.

Why should you listen to me when I talk about desktop publishing? I bring to this book my fairly unique perspective as both a designer and a bit-head. On the one hand, I've designed and produced everything from books and magazines to business cards and newsletters. And on the other, I've programmed computers, taught people how to use them, and even taken them apart for fun.

WHY I WROTE THIS BOOK

I wrote this book for three reasons. First, there isn't enough communication between the technical gurus and the design gurus. They have a lot to learn from each other, but they get caught up because they don't always know each others' terminology or concerns. Second, the gurus always seem to talk on a level that normal people can't understand, and then get frustrated when someone doesn't "get it." This book "talks" in plain English, and it never gets frustrated with you.

The third reason I wrote this book is because I didn't want you to suffer like I did. What's a corrupted font? Why would you want to kern type, anyway? How can paragraph styles change your life? This book answers these questions (and many more) that my mother (and probably yours) never even thought of.

ORGANIZATION

Each chapter of the book covers a different area of desktop publishing. You don't have to read the chapters in order, if you don't want to. In fact, if you need to bone up on a particular subject, you can easily read just that chapter. The opening page of each chapter contains a list of what's inside. This outline of the chapter is useful as a mini table of contents and for reviewing what you've read.

WHAT YOU SHOULD KNOW

In order to get the most out of this book, you should be fluent in Macintosh terminology. You need to know what the Command and Option keys are, what clicking and dragging a mouse does, and how to use menus, dialog boxes, and the basic operating system. All of this information is described in great detail in Apple's manuals.

This book is not a how-to, step-by-step kind of book like what you might be used to in computer books. I cover the essentials of desktop publishing from the ground up. I call it "electronic publishing theory." Other people tell me that they call it "just good stuff to know." Whatever it is, I hope you enjoy it.

THE CHAPTERS

Here's a rundown of what's in each chapter.

Graphic File Formats. If the differences between TIFF and EPSF or PICT and PNTG ever confused you, or if you don't understand the basic difference between bitmapped images and object-oriented (outline) images, this chapter is a great place to start. I also cover the use of the Clipboard, and answer a question about why you can't copy graphics from some applications into others.

Fonts. If you use text on the Macintosh, you're using fonts. Without a strong grasp of what screen and printer fonts are and how to use them properly, it's almost impossible to hack your way through the treacherous jungle vines of font conflicts, type rendering, and typeface selection. Type 1, Type 3, and TrueType fonts are also covered here.

Word Processing. Perhaps Robin Williams said it best when she titled her book *The Mac Is Not a Typewriter.* This chapter looks at how and why you can't treat your computer as if you were typing on a typewriter or using a pen. I cover topics such as word wrap, glossaries, proportional fonts, and special characters. The chapter ends with a discussion of the importance and techniques of copy editing.

Typography. There's text and then there's type. If you don't understand the difference between the two, or if you want to learn more about issues such as typefaces, kerning, leading, and typographic color, Chapter 5, *Typography,* can help. I also cover character formatting, paragraph formatting, widows and orphans, and page grids, in detail. Plenty of illustrations, too!

Styles & Codes. Paragraph styles (style sheets) are one of the single most important features of a desktop publishing package. However, few people ever master them, and even fewer use them efficiently. This chapter shows you how you can save hundreds of hours of work by simply letting the computer do what it's good at. This chapter also includes a discussion of code-based typesetting systems and why they're not entirely outmoded.

Scans & Halftones. Here we take a quick step backward to the world of bitmapped images. This section is important if you use photographic scans or synthetic bitmapped images (from programs like Adobe Photoshop or DeskPaint). The second part of the chapter covers halftoning (the method of printing grays on a black-and-white printer). The last section covers OCR software and why it does or doesn't work.

Color. If you work with color or are considering working with color on a Macintosh, this chapter is for you. In it, I discuss color models (such as RGB, CMYK, and Trumatch), and spot color versus process color. I also explain why the color you see on your screen rarely has anything to do with what comes out of a printer, and why you need to think about trapping and overprinting colors.

Printing. This chapter pretty much wraps up the desktop publishing theory part of the book. In it, I cover the Chooser, the Page Setup dialog box, and the Print dialog box, as well as color separation and registration marks. I end the chapter with an in-depth look at what you need to know when working with a service bureau.

When Things Go Worng. Inevitably, something goes wrong, especially when you need it most to go right. This chapter gives you an overview of what could go wrong with your software and hardware, and how you might fix it. Topics include strange beeps, printing problems, and corrupted files. This chapter was written from the sweat of too much experience with "weirdness."

Software. This may be the most biased chapter in the book. In it, I discuss what I look for when buying software, plus what programs are on my "must-have" list. This chapter also includes descriptions of the programs on the Survival Kit disk included in the back of the book.

Glossary and Index. The last section in the book contains a glossary and an index. If you're looking for a definition or a reminder of what something is, this is the first place to go. In it, you'll find both a detailed description of the item, and an index to pages where you can find out more about it.

THE QUARKXPRESS BOOK

Some of you may have read a book I co-authored called *The QuarkXPress Book*. If you're a careful reader, you'll notice that there are a few sections and illustrations that have been duplicated here in this book. Why my editor and publisher let me get away with this, I'll never know. But I'll tell you the two reasons why I did it.

First and foremost, the information that I copied was written so well (in my humble opinion) that I couldn't figure out any way to write it better.

The second reason is that the information is basic to desktop publishing, and it needed saying in both books.

ACKNOWLEDGMENTS

Remember what your third-grade teacher said? "Never judge a book by its cover." Well, the cover of *The Desktop Publisher's Survival Kit* has my name on it, but that only tells part of the story. I'd like to thank some other people who made this book possible.

First, many thanks go to the team of editors and production folks who worked very hard to get this book finished: Steve Roth and Susie Hammond (my editors, officemates, and friends) of Open House; Cindy Bell, whose eagle eye saved us from some perilous blunders; and Mike Arst, whose fingers move like wind over the keyboard. The cover design was by Ark and Vadim at Studio Silicon, and the book's interior design came from the illustrious Olav Martin Kvern, who never ceases to amaze me. Thanks also to Doug Peltonen, Don Sellers, Sarah Norman, and Leslie Simons for their feedback and support. And to Harvard Espresso for the best espresso mocha in Seattle.

Thanks to Ted, Gregor, Keasley, and Gaen (among others) at Peachpit Press, the coolest publishing house with the hottest books. And my heartfelt appreciation goes to my family, to Don Munsil, to Debbie Carlson, and to baby Jesse (who couldn't quite reach the keyboard to help make pages yet).

David Blatner
Seattle, 1991

CHAPTER 2

GRAPHIC FILE FORMATS

WHAT'S INSIDE

▶ Graphic images are saved in various formats on the Macintosh, including Paint, PICT, EPSF, and TIFF. Formats are either bitmapped or object-oriented.

▶ Bitmapped image file formats describe a picture as a grid of pixels, or dots. Bitmapped images are described by their dimensions, resolution, and pixel depth.

▶ Object-oriented file formats describe a picture as a collection of objects, such as lines, circles, and text.

▶ The Macintosh Clipboard has limits as to what file formats it can transfer from one application to another.

7

I recently had a business partner and a mutual friend over for dinner. I thought we were all having a fine time until I saw our friend yawn, and I realized that she hadn't talked since the topic of conversation had turned to an illustrated catalog that we were producing.

"It's not that what you're talking about isn't interesting," she later told me. "It's just that you're talking in some foreign language that they didn't offer at my school."

The "foreign language" that she referred to is the language of Macintosh graphic file formats, and it can easily sound as strange as ancient Greek to the uneducated ear. These file formats have names such as EPS, EPSF, EPSP, TIFF, RIFF, PICT, PICT2, PNTG, compressed TIFF, MacPaint, and Draw. Some of these are different names for the same thing, others are subtly different, and a few represent totally different concepts. In this chapter, we look at what each of these names means and discuss when you should use them in your work.

The fundamental question concerning a graphic file on the Macintosh is whether it is bitmapped or object-oriented. In the following two sections, I talk about these two formats in some detail. If it starts sounding too complex, just take a deep breath and try it again. It's worth working through the text to get the ideas behind it.

BITMAPS

Bitmapped images are the most common type of file format. When you use a scanner and scanning software, you are generating a bitmapped image. When you use an image-editing or paint program such as Adobe Photoshop, MacPaint, or ImageStudio, you are working with and generating bitmapped images. However, no matter how ubiquitous bitmapped images are, you are still strictly limited as to how you can use them.

Bitmapped images are just that: images made of mapped bits. A bit is a small piece of information. To begin with, let's think of it as a single pixel, or dot, which can be turned on or off (later we'll see that one bit doesn't always equal one pixel). When you look very closely at the screen of a black-and-white Macintosh, you can see that the screen image is made up of thousands of these tiny bits. Some are turned on (black), and some are turned off (white). The "map" is the computer's internal blueprint of the image: "Bit number 1 is turned on, bit number 2 is turned off," and so on (see Figure 2-1).

There are three primary pieces of information that are relevant to any bitmapped image: its dimensions, resolution, and pixel depth.

FIGURE 2-1
Bitmaps are
maps of bits

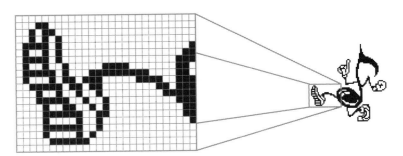

Dimensions. The bitmap is a rectangular area that describes every dot (pixel) in and around the image. This area is broken down into a grid of many square pixels. Every pixel is whole and not fractured. You can describe the dimensions of the gridded area in several ways, but it is most often specified by the number of squares or pixels per side.

For example, you might hear of a "640-by-480-pixel" image (often the size of a video screen capture), or a "72-by-72-pixel" image. Note that we can't tell the size in inches or centimeters by these numbers, because we don't know how many pixels there are per inch. The same video image can be displayed on a 9-inch or a 36-inch television screen, and a 72-by-72-pixel image could be 1 inch wide or 3 feet wide. It all depends on the image's resolution.

Resolution. The resolution of the bitmapped image is usually defined as the number of pixels, or squares, per inch on the grid (or course, this is different in countries using the metric system).

Resolution is often talked about in dots per inch (dpi). Note that the higher the resolution, the smaller each pixel is. That is, at 100 dots per inch, each pixel is ¹⁄₁₀₀ inch in size. At 10 dpi, each pixel is much larger (¹⁄₁₀ inch).

Resolution is tied directly to how big the image is on screen or on paper. For example, a 72-by-72-pixel image at a resolution of 72 dots per inch is 1 inch wide and 1 inch tall. If you're like a friend of mine who blanks out everything that deals with numbers, you should read over the last sentence several times until you really get it.

72 dots per inch is fairly low resolution. Other common resolutions are 144 dpi, 300 dpi, and 600 dpi (see Figure 2-2). Some slide scanners scan images at more than 4,000 dots per inch! Although resolution affects how rough or smooth an image appears to be, let's hold off for just a little while to talk about how.

Pixel depth. Each pixel is not only a particular size (as determined by resolution), but also a particular color. The range of colors available is determined by the type of bitmapped image it is. In the simplest bitmapped images, each pixel is defined as either black or

FIGURE 2-2
Resolution of a
bitmapped
image

36 dpi   72 dpi

150 dpi   300 dpi

white. These are called 1-bit images because each pixel is described with one bit of information. They are also known as bilevel images because that one bit can be turned either on or off (signified by 1 or 0). Bilevel images are flat; they have no depth.

Earlier I mentioned that one pixel might be defined by more than one bit of information. Now we see why. One-bit images can only describe one of two colors (black or white, on or off). Two-bit images, where each pixel is described with two bits of information, can describe four colors or levels of gray. Anything more than a 1-bit image is called a deep bitmap. For example, an 8-bit image is deep because it can describe up to 256 (2^8) colors or shades of gray for each pixel (those of us in the Northwest, having to look at gray a lot, can identify and name most of those shades). A 24-bit image can describe over 16 million colors (see Figure 2-3).

When you're working with bitmapped images, it's important to know and understand their dimensions, resolution, and pixel depth. For example, an 8-bit, 72-dpi, 100-by-100-pixel image is going to act and look very differently from a 24-bit, 266-dpi, 600-by-300-pixel image. Let's look at why.

FIGURE 2-3
Pixel depth determines the number of gray levels

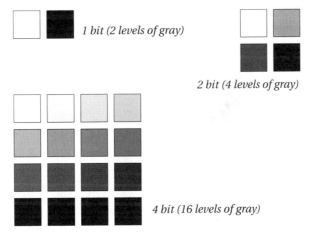

1 bit (2 levels of gray)

2 bit (4 levels of gray)

4 bit (16 levels of gray)

WORKING
WITH
BITMAPPED
IMAGES

The limitations inherent in bitmapped images become obvious when you manipulate the picture in some way, such as enlarging it significantly. The key is that the picture's resolution is related directly to its size. If you double the size of a bitmap, you cut its resolution in half; if you reduce the picture to one-quarter its size, you multiply its resolution by four. For example, a 72-dpi, 1-bit graphic when enlarged 200 percent becomes a twice-as-rough 36-dpi image. However, when reduced to 50 percent, it becomes a less-jaggy 144-dpi image (see Figure 2-4).

A gray-scale or color image, when enlarged, becomes pixelated, rather than looking "rougher." That is, you begin to see each square pixel and its tonal value (see Figure 2-5).

The key here is that no matter how large or small you make an image, you're never really adding or subtracting any pixels.

Bitmapped images are especially good for photorealistic and three-dimensional images because of the level of detail and spectrum of coloring and shading you can achieve. Magazines such as *Verbum* and *Pixel Vision* show this nicely.

OBJECT-ORIENTED GRAPHICS

Instead of describing a picture bit by bit, object-oriented graphic file formats specify each element of a picture by means of a coordinate system. Whereas a bitmapped file could take an enormous amount

FIGURE 2-4
Reducing or enlarging a bilevel bitmapped image changes its printed resolution

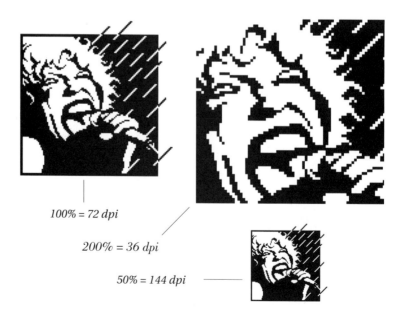

100% = 72 dpi

200% = 36 dpi

50% = 144 dpi

FIGURE 2-5
Reducing or
enlarging a gray-
level bitmapped
image can cause
pixelation

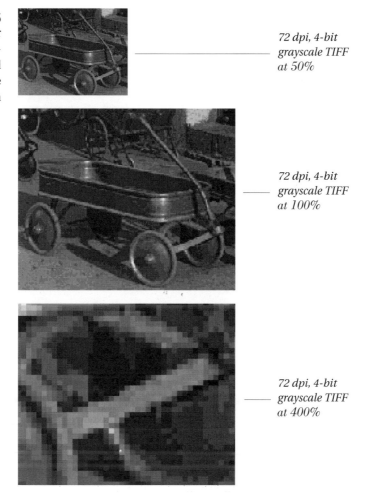

*72 dpi, 4-bit
grayscale TIFF
at 50%*

*72 dpi, 4-bit
grayscale TIFF
at 100%*

*72 dpi, 4-bit
grayscale TIFF
at 400%*

of memory to describe one circle, an object-oriented file could describe it in one line: "Draw a circle of this size with a center at X,Y." The computer knows what a circle is, and how to create it. Different object-oriented file formats can describe different things, but most can easily specify objects such as straight lines, curves, and type, as well as attributes such as shading and object rotation angle. These files are almost always created by an illustration program such as MacDraw, FreeHand, or Illustrator.

Most object-oriented graphic files can also contain bitmapped images as objects in their own right. However, note that illustration programs usually can't edit bitmapped images (just as paint programs cannot usually edit object-oriented graphic images).

The magic of object-oriented graphic images is that you can stretch them, rotate them, twist them into pastry, and print them on various resolution printers without worrying about how smoothly the lines will print. When you print on a 300-dpi plain-paper laser printer, you get a full 300 dots per inch, and when you print to film with a 3,000-dpi printer, you get beautifully smooth lines at 3,000 dots per inch! There is no inherent limit of information for the picture, as there is in bitmaps (see Figure 2-6). Theoretically, there are no inherent limits to the number of gray levels in an object-oriented picture. Realistically, however, each format has upper limits.

FILE TYPES

Now that we've covered the basics of graphic file formats, let's jump in and look at the specific file formats on the Macintosh. On the Macintosh, each file is identified by its "type." When I talk about file types in this book, I'm talking about two things: how the information is formatted within the file, and how the file is saved on disk. The common usage of the term "file type" refers to the way in which the file's information is formatted (as in a MacPaint file). Then there is the way the Macintosh system names files when it saves them to disk: it gives every file an actual, technical, four-letter file type. For

FIGURE 2-6
Object-oriented
graphics are
different from
bitmapped
graphics

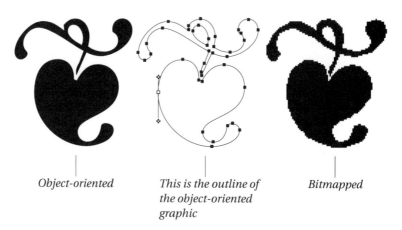

Object-oriented   *This is the outline of*   *Bitmapped*
                         the object-oriented
                         graphic

instance, files generally referred to as "Paint" or "MacPaint" files are type PNTG. For the sake of simplicity, we use the terms "type" and "format" interchangeably.

You can determine any file's type using one of several different utilities, such as CE Software's DiskTop (our favorite utility for this sort of task; see Figure 2-7). It's critical for a desktop publisher to understand and be able to identify file types. The discussion below covers the main graphic file formats used on the Macintosh (see Table 2-1 for a summary).

Paint/PNTG. The Paint format is ultimately the most basic of all graphic formats on the Macintosh. When the Mac first shipped in 1984, it came with two programs: MacWrite and MacPaint. The latter was a very basic paint program that let you create bitmapped images, cutting and pasting these pictures into MacWrite files, or saving them as Paint-format (PNTG) files.

Paint files are black and white (1 bit), 72 dots per inch, 8 by 10 inches (576 by 720 pixels). That's it. No more and no less. Even text is handled like a bitmapped graphic image; the only way to edit text is to edit the pixels that make it up. Clearly, this format has some stringent limitations which restrict the usability of the images. You can see examples of PNTG files from T/Maker Software on the Survival Kit disk (see Chapter 11, *Software*).

PICT graphics. The PICT format, also a part of the original Mac system, but first made easy to use with MacDraw, tackles graphic

FIGURE 2-7
DiskTop lets you see and change file type and creator

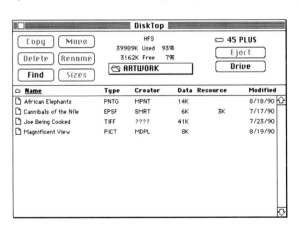

TABLE 2-1
Graphic file
types

Name	Type	Kind	Description
Paint	PNTG	bitmap	1 bit, 72 dpi, 8 by 10 inches; very basic images
PICT	PICT	bitmap or object	1 bit, any resolution or dimension; object-oriented PICTs should be avoided
PICT2	PICT	bitmap or object	any dimension, resolution, or pixel depth; object-oriented PICT2s should be avoided
PICT/EPS	Clipboard	object	PICT file on the clipboard that has EPS comments; when you print, the printer uses the EPS information instead of the PICT image
EPSF	EPSF	object	any size, some limits to complexity; often has bitmapped image for screen preview
TIFF	TIFF	bitmap	any dimension, resolution, or pixel depth; best format for bitmapped images

images on an object level as opposed to a bitmap level. However, a PICT image can contain bitmaps either alongside an object-oriented drawing, or as its only object ("bitmap-only PICTs").

PICT images can be any size, but only black and white (gray levels, just as in MacPaint documents, are handled by a dithered bitmap pattern to simulate gray). PICT2 images—which because of their ubiquity are now simply called PICT images—support color and gray scales.

Ultimately, the biggest problem with the PICT format is its unreliability in several respects. For example, line widths can change when moving a picture from one program to another, and text spacing can change, sometimes drastically. Also, printing to high-resolution printers (1,200+ dpi) can be spotty. Remember that when you print a PICT to a PostScript imagesetter, the computer has to convert from one object-oriented language to another. I trust these conversions about as far as I can throw them. Nonetheless, PICT (including PICT2) is the primary format for printing to non-PostScript devices.

For the sake of completeness, we should note that it is also possible to attach a PostScript description of the image to a PICT image (see "The Clipboard," below).

Encapsulated PostScript or EPSF. Encapsulated PostScript format (EPSF or EPS) is certainly the most reliable format for putting images on paper or film. PostScript is a powerful object-oriented page-description language, though its files may contain noneditable bitmaps as well. Although it has built-in font-handling features, it ultimately treats type as a graphic made of lines and curves. This makes working with fonts in a PostScript environment a joy, with many possibilities (see Chapter 3, *Fonts*). It is easy to create a PostScript file on the Macintosh, but to print it out you must have a PostScript-compatible printer, such as an Apple Laserwriter II or a Ricoh PC6000/PS.

Encapsulated PostScript is simply a PostScript file with two extra features. The first feature is an internal comment that tells the Macintosh how large the image is, and where it's positioned on the page (this is called its bounding box).

The second feature is a low-resolution bitmapped image that you can see on the screen when you import it into a program like PageMaker, QuarkXPress, or WordPerfect. This image acts as a representative to the underlying PostScript information, so when the file is printed to a PostScript printer, the bitmap is ignored and the underlying PostScript is used. If this preview image—which is generally a PICT or TIFF file—is not included, then you just see a big gray box on the screen, which may contain some basic information such as the file's name. For example, preview images wouldn't be included on most EPSF files that were created on a mainframe computer and ported over to the Macintosh.

One nice thing about EPS files (and PostScript in general), is that they are written as text files that you can open with a word processor (see Figure 2-8). If you know PostScript, you can then edit the

FIGURE 2-8
PostScript

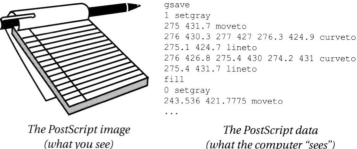

```
gsave
1 setgray
275 431.7 moveto
276 430.3 277 427 276.3 424.9 curveto
275.1 424.7 lineto
276 426.8 275.4 430 274.2 431 curveto
275.4 431.7 lineto
fill
0 setgray
243.536 421.7775 moveto
   ...
```

The PostScript image
(what you see)

The PostScript data
(what the computer "sees")

file, changing what the picture looks like. I've included some EPS clip art from 3G Graphics on the Survival Kit disk (see Chapter 11, *Software*).

TIFF. The Tagged Image File Format (TIFF) is another form of bitmap. However, it has significantly more potential to produce high-quality images than PNTG bitmapped images. First off, instead of the standard 8-by-10-inch, 72-dpi, black-and-white PNTG image, a TIFF file can be created with any dimensions and resolution, and can include gray-scale or color information. It is important to remember that these images are still just big bitmaps, and therefore only contain a finite amount of information (see Figure 2-9).

Nonetheless, because of the flexibility of TIFF files, most scanning and image-editing programs such as DeskScan, ImageStudio, and Adobe Photoshop save and open the TIFF format. I've included a TIFF image on the Survival Kit disk that you can look at (see Chapter 11, *Software*).

TIFF files can seem simple until you really need to work with them in a variety of environments. As it turns out, there are several different TIFF formats, including compressed and uncompressed TIFF, CMYK and RGB TIFF, and RIFF (Raster Image File Format—this isn't really a TIFF file, but for the sake of brevity, we've included it here). Plus, TIFF files from an IBM PC are usually different from Macintosh TIFFs. What does all this mean? Only that you may encounter stumbling blocks when bringing certain TIFF images into the software of your choice.

For example, I recently worked on a project where we brought TIFF images from a PC to a Macintosh and tried to get them into

FIGURE 2-9
TIFF format

```
Ÿ›‰ÏÓÒÛÙ0ÛÛÛ§≠√,,‹»Ω¥úèÇxuqd_]ivâü§¶≠≠¿ƒƒ¡¡¡¬
¿π´¶§óìóóóóúöñââçêíóú°ôêçãã∩̃Âzty{~áá∩̃sosoieQQ
MHFHMHFCIIFB@A?@@<=?AO[`YZWexÉÜâèâêõ£•±ª¿À–
ŸÁÈÏÚÛ0ÚÛÛù¶∂ŸŸ"øπ¥òã{nd]MHHOVcty} Çóöôóõòöóê{
yzpoquuswtnefkkmty}smjhedf][_`dnpjYZ]ZTP@>>>9
<@<67??<8775;97;;;FOTQOO^v~Ã0̃àçÑãèì£Æ≥Ω¬Ôfl‰È
ÚÙÚÛŒ…∏¶¨ßµ√ƒòs^F<6,,*+,134568@CCCLIKJLF>>>
?>CFC=<<;==<97=>@>?A<>@8=HGB?<;=@@732.,//-
++,++.25;8785664324>HIC@[oxxvxsvw{~àë0°™∑»À'
‡Ï0Óî`À∂êêëÆV…ïhR=6/(((,+/114139<>CKJIGH@75?A
@ACB>=;998=;658;<@B=
....
```

The TIFF image   The TIFF data
(what you see)   (what the computer "sees")

QuarkXPress. No go. However, we could bring them into Enhance, save them, open them in Adobe Photoshop, save them again, and *then* bring them into QuarkXPress. It was frustrating (especially for 258 different images!), but it finally worked, and that's what was important. I discuss these sorts of problems—and more—in Chapter 10, *When Things Go Worng.*

THE CLIPBOARD

The Macintosh system has a storage area called the Clipboard that lets you take information from one place and put it somewhere else. Whenever you cut, copy, or paste, you're using the Clipboard. Thus, you can cut or copy a picture from one application into the Clipboard, and then paste it from the Clipboard into another application.

However, there's a limit to the flexibility of the Clipboard. For example, you'll find that you can't copy an illustration directly from FreeHand and paste it into Microsoft Word or Adobe Illustrator. This is because Word and Illustrator don't understand FreeHand's PostScript outline format. They do, however, understand the PICT/EPS format, among other types. You can create a PICT/EPS version of an object within Illustrator or FreeHand by holding down the Option key while selecting Cut or Copy from the menu. This places the PICT/EPS image on the Clipboard.

You can also use the Scrapbook (on the Apple menu) in conjunction with cutting and pasting to bring over several objects at a time by cutting or copying an object, opening the Scrapbook, pasting it in, and then repeating the process for each object you want. If you have copied an object from FreeHand or Illustrator using the Option key technique described above, it is not necessary to hold down the Option key to copy it out of the Scrapbook and back onto the Clipboard.

HOW TO USE GRAPHIC FILES

Far be it from me to tell you what kinds of pictures you should use and where you should use them! But I will give you some guidelines for how to use these files.

Importing files. One question that I often hear is, "How do I get these pictures into my program?" I don't mean to be unfair, but my response is generally: "Read the program manual." Each program can import and export certain file types, and they aren't always what you'd expect or want. For example, you can't open a TIFF file in Illustrator, but you can use its Place command to import an EPS file. PageMaker can directly import some types of TIFF files (using the Place command) that QuarkXPress can't (using the Get Picture command), and QuarkXPress can import RIFF, which almost no other program can.

Converting file formats. There is, however, some hope in all this file format mess: file conversion. Programs are just now coming out that convert one file type to another. For example, GoScript converts EPS to TIFF files, though it uses a PostScript clone interpreter to do it. (Does the sound of that make you nervous? It should; see "Post-Script" in Chapter 9, *Printing*.) Adobe Photoshop and Color Studio's Shapes annex now also read Illustrator files and some other EPS files, and can convert them to TIFF images. You have to be careful with conversion utilities, though. For example, there's a little DA floating around the electronic bulletin board systems that purports to convert EPS files to PICT format. However, all it really does is remove the low-resolution PICT preview image from the file and put it on the Clipboard (this is sometimes handy, but it's not really converting the file).

Photoshop can open a TIFF file and save it as EPS. Or, if you want to get really adventurous, you can import a TIFF file into QuarkXPress or PageMaker, overlay type on it, and export the whole page as an EPS file.

THESE THINGS WON'T WORK

Although I hate to end a chapter talking about a few things you can't do rather than all the things you can, I do think it's important that we cover this stuff. So here it is: a quick list of things you needn't bother trying.

▶ Double-clicking on an EPS or any other kind of graphic file won't show you its preview image. You need to import it into another program to see it.

▶ There's almost no way that any program can do anything to an EPS picture other than scale it, rotate it, or skew it. You can't change the colors in the EPS, and you can't alter text that's embedded in the file (remember that EPS files are encapsulated, which means they're almost totally "locked" to any change).

▶ You can't change a picture's file type using ResEdit or Disktop. The only way to get an EPSF from a TIFF is to either trace it with a program like Streamline (which converts it into an object-oriented PostScript file) or open it in a program like Photoshop and save it as an EPS (which simply saves it as a bitmap-only EPS).

CHAPTER 3

FONTS

WHAT'S INSIDE

▶ Macintosh fonts and typefaces are electronic files that describe the overall look of a set of characters.

▶ A screen font is a set of bitmapped images—one image for each character at a specific size.

▶ A printer font is a set of object-oriented outline images. However, each outline can be "stretched" to any size.

▶ The three types of printer fonts are Type 1, Type 3, and TrueType.

▶ Type rendering uses the printer font's outlines to create high-quality bitmapped images for the screen or for a non-PostScript printer.

If you have no intention of using any sort of text in your work, you can just go ahead and skip this chapter. The rest of us are going to take a careful look at how text and type are handled on the Macintosh. First we're going to learn the tools of typography. Then (in Chapter 5, *Typography*) we're going to actually use them. Notice that I'm not jumping immediately to *My Favorite Tips for Precision Typographic Excellence*. It's kind of like music. First you have to understand all those little marks on the page. Then you can sit down and play Mozart, Chopin, or John Cage's *4' 33"*.

Remember, this chapter has all the information that you really need to know to get the job done. However, there are so many font issues that you could write a book about them. In fact, Erfert Fenton already did: *The Macintosh Font Book* (available from Peachpit Press) is an excellent resource for further information about fonts.

Before we look at fonts, we need to look at two issues: the terminology we're using, and ASCII text.

Words, words, words... My editor and I keep getting into the same argument over the naming conventions used in typography. Historically, the word typeface was used to describe the overall look of the type (its particular combination of curves and strokes), while font was used to describe a character set at a particular size. For example, the words you're reading are in the typeface Utopia, while the headings are in the font 18-point Lithos Black. That's how Steve uses the terminology. I like the present-day common usage, in which font and typeface are interchangeable terms. That is, the words you're reading are printed in one typeface (font), and the headings to each section are in another font (typeface).

While editors get to make a lot of decisions throughout a book, this is one that I'm sticking to. So from now on, when I talk about a font or a typeface, you'll know I'm talking about the same thing.

Font families (like people families) are usually three or four separate fonts that go together. For example, Times Roman is one font, Times Italic is another, Times Bold is a third, and Times Bold Italic is a fourth. All together they make the Times family.

Mac text. Plain ol' text, no styling, no formatting, no nothing, is called ASCII text. Technically, if you're interested, ASCII (pronounced "ass´-key") text is a standard way that computers code each character, so that a lower-case "a" is represented by the number 97, "b" by 98, and so on. Standards like this are important when you move text from a Macintosh to a PC, because both computers "understand" the same codes, so you get what you want.

If you're transferring text from one type of computer to another (like from a PC to a Mac), you probably want to transfer ASCII text. This becomes important later in Chapter 6, *Styles & Codes*.

MAC FONTS

Okay, now we can get to the good stuff: the wild world of Macintosh fonts. Fonts come in all sorts of forms: cast in metal, carved in wood, on photographic negatives. On the Mac, fonts are digital. This means that each character of a typeface is described electronically in a file (or files) on a disk. To get the typeface onto your screen or page, the computer has to find this file and get the appropriate information out of it.

As it turns out, in all system versions prior to System 7 (we'll look at how System 7 handles fonts later in the chapter), the Macintosh puts font characters on the screen in a different way than it prints them on a laser printer. Therefore, there are two types of font-description files on the Mac: screen fonts ("bitmapped fonts") and printer fonts ("outline fonts").

SCREEN FONTS

Screen fonts are collections of bitmapped images—one bitmapped image for each character at a particular size (if you don't know the difference between bitmapped and outline graphics, take a quick peek at Chapter 2, *Graphic File Formats*). When you type a key on the keyboard, the computer goes to the screen font file, pulls out the bitmapped image for that character, and puts it on the screen.

The problem with bitmapped fonts, though, is that they're set up to be used only at a specific size and resolution. For example, the font New York 12 is designed to be printed at 12 points at 72 dots per inch. If you want 13-point New York, the computer just enlarges New York 12, which is pretty ugly (see Figure 3-1).

FIGURE 3-1
Screen fonts
get jaggy at
odd sizes

Helvetica Condensed at 12 point

Helvetica Condensed at 28 point

Similarly, if you print a bitmapped screen font on a 300-dpi printer, it only prints at 72 dpi. This, too, looks "stair-steppy" (though some people use that as a design style).

Screen fonts aren't only used for the screen. The Mac also uses them to print to the ImageWriter dot-matrix printer, the LaserWriter SC, and some inkjet printers.

Loading screen fonts. Screen fonts are stored in suitcases (this is evident by their perpetually rumpled look, which some people call "jaggy"). There are three methods of loading fonts so that you can use them.

1. The first is by using Font/DA Mover to move the fonts out of their suitcases and into the System file. (As an exercise, go ahead and open your System Folder and locate the System file; most people don't know it's even there, but that's half of what makes the computer go!)

2. If you're using System 7, you can install screen fonts without the Font/DA Mover: just drag the font icon on top of the System file (which acts as a folder for fonts).

3. The third method is to use a utility such as MasterJuggler or Suitcase II. Unless you aren't working with many fonts, the third method is much preferred, for two reasons.

   ▶ Moving many fonts around with Font/DA Mover can screw up both the fonts and your System file, in the long run.

   ▶ Moving fonts in and out of the System 7 file is inefficient (if there's anything that drives me crazy, it's inefficiency).

PRINTER FONTS

If the Mac uses screen fonts on the screen, then it must use printer fonts for printers (except for the ImageWriter and other non-PostScript devices). And whereas the screen font is bitmapped, the characters in a printer font are described as object-oriented outline graphics that can be scaled, rotated, and skewed in all sorts of ways without the ugly, jaggy extrapolation encountered on the screen.

There are three types of printer fonts that you should be aware of: Type 1, Type 3, and TrueType.

Type 1. If you've been working in desktop publishing for a while, you've probably been working with Type 1 fonts. These are the PostScript outline fonts that Adobe, Monotype, Bitstream, and other major font vendors produce. They're the most compact fonts in size, and they're encrypted so that even if you knew PostScript, it would be difficult for you to "crack the code" and play with the data. The most important thing about Type 1 fonts is their hinting. Hinting is the process that makes fonts look good at small sizes on low-resolution printers (like desktop laser printers). Figure 3-2 shows an example of why hinting is good.

FIGURE 3-2
TrueType fonts can align to the screen or printer pixels for better-looking type

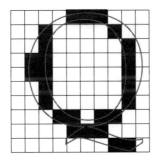 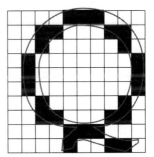

Type 3. The second type of PostScript outline font, Type 3, looks exactly the same as a Type 1 font when it's printed to a high-resolution imagesetter. However, it lacks the hinting mechanisms that make Type 1 fonts look so good on lower-resolution printers. They're also often slightly larger in file size (which most people don't really care about, in these days of 120 mb hard drives).

For the first four years of PostScript fonts, only professional font companies could create Type 1 fonts. Type 3 fonts could be created by anyone who purchased Altsys' Fontographer, so there were a lot of pretty cruddy fonts being sold or given away (it's not Altsys' fault; they've got a great tool, but people use it poorly). It's not surprising, therefore, that Type 3 fonts have fallen out of favor with most designers and ad agencies, and have taken firm hold only in the underground font collector's disk collection.

Now, Fontographer or Letraset's FontStudio can create both Type 1 or Type 3 fonts, and people are converting those cruddy Type 3 fonts into Type 1 and back again; and the only way to know what the good fonts are is to read Clifford Burke's or Kathleen Tinkel's font columns in various magazines, or (what most people do) still keep buying from the large manufacturers (and even then you need to be careful, or else how will you know whether to buy Futura from Bitstream or from Adobe?).

TrueType. So it appears that a couple of years ago, Microsoft Corp. and Apple Corp. were sitting around having lunch, and they decided that Adobe was charging too much for their PostScript font technology. Their answer was to create TrueType—their own font technology (then code-named "Royal"). Some people thought this was the worst mistake the companies had ever made. Others thought it would be a great boon to the font industry and make desktop publishers feel better than James Brown. The answer, it seems, is mixed, at best.

TrueType fonts are outline fonts that rely on a totally different set of mathematical functions than PostScript fonts. They're hinted, but their hinting is performed differently than in Type 1 fonts. While Type 1 fonts rely on a "smart PostScript printer" to figure out how they should be hinted, TrueType fonts have all their hinting information built into the font itself.

It's like the difference between bringing your own toppings to a pizza parlor or letting the pizza chefs use their own. TrueType fonts carry their own special toppings (hints) around with them, and almost any PostScript printer can use them to make a great-tasting pizza. Type 1 fonts rely on the printer to have the toppings they want; in other words, they'll only work on a PostScript printer. But the pizza tastes just as good either way.

To work with TrueType fonts on the Macintosh, you must either work in System 7 or with the TrueType INIT that Apple released to user groups and included with their non-PostScript printers.

At the time of this writing, TrueType fonts have not proven themselves to be worth working with, and I've stuck with Type 1 fonts. There do seem to be some benefits to using TrueType on the PC Windows side of things, but that's not what we're here to talk about.

WHAT TO DO WITH PRINTER FONTS

There are two things you can do with a Type 1, Type 3, or TrueType printer font: install it for use, and transform it into something else.

Installing printer fonts. Installing a printer font is about as easy as it gets: just drag it into your System Folder. If you use MasterJuggler or Suitcase II, you can keep the printer font in the same folder as your screen fonts. I have a folder that has all my screen and printer fonts in it (I have lots). When I need a font, I use MasterJuggler to access the screen font. The Mac can then find the printer font on its own.

Transmogrification. So you've found the perfect font for the job, but it's a TrueType font and you've sworn off TrueType. Or perhaps you own a Type 1 PostScript font, but don't have ATM (discussed below) or a PostScript printer. No problem! You can use utilities like FontMonger from Ares Software, or Metamorphosis Professional from Altsys Corporation, to change one font type into another. These programs also perform tricks like turning a character in a font into an EPS outline so you can use it in an illustration program.

ON THE MENUS

Whenever you have a font loaded, you can access it from a menu in the application you're running. For example, in PageMaker you can access the font from the Font submenu. However, how the font looks on the menu and how you should choose it depends on how you have your system set up.

For example, if you have the most basic setup on the Macintosh, your font menus probably contain font names like LBI Helvetica Black Oblique and SbI 2Stone Sans SemibdItal. You can change these by using an INIT like Adobe Type Reunion—which combines font families into hierarchical menus (I hate h-menus, so I avoid this program)—or Fontina, which reduces the size of all the font names to fit onto the screen at one time.

I'm often asked how people should choose styled fonts, such as bold or italic. For example, should people choose BI Times Bold Italic or just choose Times and then apply a bold and italic style to it? I always suggest choosing the base font and applying styles to it. This is for two reasons.

▶ It's easy to change fonts quickly while retaining local formatting. For example, if you change a single word in a paragraph to Times Italic, then change the paragraph's style (see Chapter 6, *Styles & Codes*) to Garamond, the entire paragraph changes to Garamond, and the italic word is no longer italic.

▶ Some programs, such as PageMaker and QuarkXPress, let you search for a word in a particular font. For example, you can search for "hat" in Garamond. If you set the word "hat" to B Garamond Bold rather than Garamond with a bold style, the program would not be able to find it when you were searching for all words "hat" that were Garamond.

FALSE STYLES

Although I cover the topic of character formatting fully in Chapter 5, *Typography*, I want to bring up a potential pitfall for the unwary: false styles. If you select a typeface and then apply a style such as bold or italic to it, unless you have a screen font or a printer font for that style, your screen display and/or printouts may not give you a true bold or italic typeface.

For example, let's say you set a line of text in Times Roman, then apply the italic style to one word. If you don't have a screen font loaded for Times Italic (most people don't), the Macintosh mathematically obliques (slants) the font for you (see Figure 3-3). This is a false italic. When you print this line of text, the italic face comes out in a true italic, because the true Times Italic printer font is resident in PostScript printers.

FIGURE 3-3
False styles

Quietly they stalked   *Original*

Quietly they stalked   *Oblique (false italic)*

Quietly they stalked   *True italic*

However, if you don't have a PostScript printer or if the printer font isn't loaded, the font does print as a false italic.

Other character styles are also handled this way. For example, false bolds are usually double struck for a darker color (this looks much worse than it sounds).

TYPE RENDERING

Okay, I lied. Screen fonts aren't the only way text is put on the screen. In fact, the low-resolution screen fonts are being used less and less these days in favor of type rendering. Type rendering is the process of the computer reading the outline information in the printer font, building a bitmapped image from the outline on the fly, and putting that on the screen. This effectively gives you a good (if not great) screen representation of a font at any size you want. Plus, you can rotate, skew, or resize the type and still get a pretty good image to work with (see Figure 3-4). On slower machines you can notice the extra time the computer takes to compute these screen images, but it's usually worth the short wait.

The first commercial program to render type was QuarkXPress, which could render most Type 3 fonts. However, most of the people who use QuarkXPress use Type 1 fonts, so it usually doesn't do them much good (though it's still the only program on the market that renders Type 3 fonts).

Next came Adobe Type Manager (ATM), which renders Type 1 fonts to the screen. If you don't already have ATM and you're using Type 1 fonts in your work, you have a homework assignment: get it.

FIGURE 3-4
Type rendering
uses the outline
font to render a
smooth screen
image

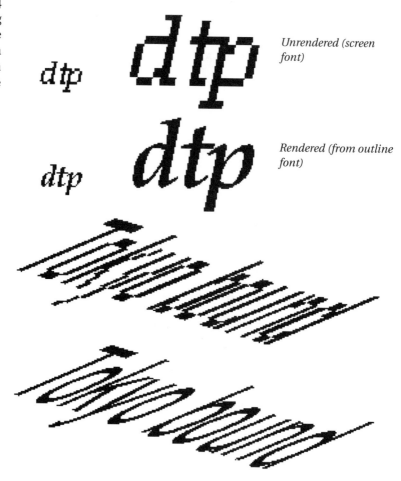

Unrendered (screen font)

Rendered (from outline font)

Now, Apple's System 7 renders TrueType images on the fly (pretty quickly, too). I suppose this method has the attraction of being free with the system, but if you use Type 1 fonts, you have to either convert them to TrueType (using a program like FontMonger, Evolution, or Metamorphosis), or use TrueType along with ATM.

In QuarkXPress and ATM you can turn type rendering on and off, relying on the faster but worse-looking bitmapped screen fonts; System 7, however, is always in rendering mode.

As it turns out, it's not just your screen image that improves with type rendering. When you print to a non-PostScript printer like an HP

DeskJet or an Apple StyleWriter, the fonts come up crisp and clean because ATM and System 7 are rendering type to the printer, too.

TYPE RENDERING AND SCREEN FONTS

You might ask, "Well, if the Mac is going to render all my printer fonts to the screen, then why should I bother with screen fonts?" As it turns out, ATM still requires you to have a screen font loaded, or else it won't be able to "find" the printer font. System 7's TrueType rendering can find a TrueType font even if you don't have a screen font loaded.

However, whether you're using Type 1 or TrueType fonts, you're probably better off with screen fonts installed for type sizes below twelve point. The screen fonts have been hand-tooled to look as good as they can, and they usually look better than the rendered versions.

FONTS AND SYSTEM 7

The great promises of System 7 were quick type rendering for the screen and printer, and two TrueType font outlines in every garage. I've met many people who are more confused by the introduction of TrueType and System 7 than relieved by it. I'm here to tell you that everything is okay; you don't have to worry about a thing.

ATM works under System 6 or System 7. TrueType works under System 7 or (with an INIT) under System 6.0.5 or higher. You can use TrueType fonts on the same page as Type 1 PostScript fonts, and as long as you don't have different fonts with the same names, you'll probably be okay.

The big difference between TrueType and PostScript fonts is that whereas you need both a screen font and a printer font for Type 1 fonts, TrueType fonts have only one file (see Figure 3-5). As I said earlier, you can install this font by dragging it into the System Folder (in System 6) or into the System file (in System 7), or—preferably—by accessing it with MasterJuggler or Suitcase II.

FIGURE 3-5
Font icons

Helve

*Type 1 printer
font from Adobe*

Helvetica

Screen font

TrueType fonts

*Screen font (in
System 7)*

Helvetica

Helvetica 10

COPYRIGHT ISSUES

I'd like to end this chapter with a quick warning regarding the copying of fonts: Don't Do It.

Although you cannot yet legally copyright a typeface design in the United States of America, the actual fonts that you're using are copyrighted. That means that they're just like software programs that you purchase. You're allowed to use them any way you want to, but you're not allowed to copy and distribute them to friends unless the font manufacturer has given you permission. You also cannot transform them into a different form and sell them as new fonts.

There are some exceptions to this rule, of course. For example, you can make copies for yourself (for archival and storage purposes). The question of whether you can loan your font to the service bureau so that it can print your files is still up in the air. However, I will say that I've never heard of anyone complaining about this practice, as long as the service bureau doesn't use that font for anything other than printing your jobs. The best solution is to send PostScript dumps of your files (see Chapter 9, *Printing*). This method can include the fonts automatically.

CHAPTER 4
WORD PROCESSING

WHAT'S INSIDE

▶ The Clipboard lets you move text and graphics around within or between documents.

▶ Word processing programs make your life better with features like find/change, word wrap, glossaries, and spell checking.

▶ The Macintosh is different from a typewriter in many ways, including proportional fonts, methods of emphasis, and special characters.

▶ A key aspect of handling text is maintaining a level of consistency in language and style. This is known as copy preparation and copyediting.

In this chapter, we're going to take a lightning-quick tour of typing on the Macintosh. I'll touch on why typing on the Mac is a different process than writing with a pen, or typing on a typewriter. Then I'll get into why and how you need to use certain techniques and working styles on the Mac. Finally, I'll make a quick diversion into the world of copyediting, where text moves from the writing stage towards page layout.

BETTER THAN PAPER?

Perhaps you've experienced it, too. For me, it was during a final exam in college. The speed at which I was accustomed to writing and rewriting, the ability to quickly move chunks of text around, even my level of creativity were all stifled when I picked up my pen and tried to write the answer to the question written on the blackboard. I knew right then than the computer really was enhancing my ability to deal with large amounts of text.

However, too often people don't let the computer do enough of their work for them. Things in this section may be obvious to some of you. Bear with me—you may discover jewels you need.

CUT, COPY, AND PASTE

The Macintosh has a very powerful feature called the Clipboard, which makes moving text and graphics around a breeze. Simply put, you can select some text or a graphic, cut or copy it, then move someplace else and paste it there.

Most of you have probably done this before, with hardly a second thought. But stop for a moment and try to visualize what's really going on. When you select Cut or Copy (or type the keyboard equivalents: Command-X or Command-C), the computer takes the selected information and stores it in the Clipboard (this is actually a file in the System Folder) in one or more formats. When you select Paste (or type Command-V), the Mac "asks" the software you're using what sort of format it will accept. For example, if you cut text from a word processor, the text will probably be saved in two formats: TEXT and RTF (Rich Text Format). If you move to an illustration program and try to paste that text, the Mac won't do anything (the illustration program doesn't understand either of those formats). On the other hand, if you select some text from Microsoft Word and type Command-Option-D, the Mac copies that text onto the Clipboard in a PICT format. MacDraw, MacPaint and FreeHand all understand this format. However, beware the dreaded PICT format, with its three heads belching unpredictable fire (see Chapter 2, *Graphic File Formats*).

Clearly, when you're copying and pasting from one program to another, you need to use common sense and—often—just try it to see what happens.

WORD POWER

Of course, word processors aren't just good at cutting and pasting. Those software engineers have come up with all sorts of ways to make our lives easier. I'll touch on four here, but these really only scratch the surface.

Find/Change. Remember that computers feel the best about themselves when they're doing things that humans can't do well. For example, searching through thousands of words, changing every occurrence of the word "whale" to "big, hunkin' fish." The technical, scientific name for this procedure is Find/Change or Find/Replace. Every word processor I can think of has this feature, and it is certainly one of the most useful in production work. Here are some examples of how I use it.

▶ Replacing all the double spaces (a typesetter's cardinal sin) with single spaces, and replacing double hyphens with em dashes.

▶ Searching and replacing for ligatures (see "Ligatures," later in this chapter) and other items on our house editorial style sheet.

▶ Searching for editor's comments; for example, my editor types "XXX" before each one of his comments in my text files. Then I just search for each occurrence of "XXX."

Word wrap. Here's another hard and fast rule: if your word processor has word wrap (just about every Macintosh program does), then type a carriage return (hard return) only at the end of a paragraph.

When you run out of room on one line, word wrap pushes you onto the next one, so there's no need to manually press the return key. The Macintosh thinks of every hard return as a new paragraph marker, so if you put hard returns in the middle of a sentence, you'll have a terrible time reformatting later. Many programs let you break to a new line without starting a new paragraph. This is called a soft return; you usually get it by typing Shift-Return.

If you are given text that has hard returns at the end of each line (this is often the case with text from an IBM machine), you can use the Add/Strip program included on the Survival Kit disk to convert them to a word wrap format (see Chapter 11, *Software*).

Glossaries. Some word-processing programs have features called "glossaries." These glossaries type a longer word or phrase for you whenever you type a shorter one. For example, if you use the word "Umbilical" a lot in Microsoft Word, you might set it up as a glossary item. Then, whenever you type Command-Backspace, then U, then Return, the Mac types the word "Umbilical" for you. You can even save whole phrases, or a paragraph or more, as glossary items.

Spelling checkers. There is no excuse anymore for misspelled wrds. Most word processing programs now have built-in spelling checkers. And, if those spelling checkers aren't good enough, or don't check the language you use, you can buy third-party utilities and dictionaries such as Thunder. Spelling checkers work by matching each word in your document with a word in their dictionary. If the program can't match your word, it asks you what you want to do about it. Most spelling checkers can give you a "best guess" as to what word they think you want.

A FISH OF A DIFFERENT COLOR

While it's true that the Macintosh computer enhances your writing and typing process, it's also true that it requires you to adapt some of your techniques to match its typographic capabilities. Why?

Because the Mac is not a pen, and the Mac is not a typewriter. Different tools, different working styles. The main issues you need to be aware of when working with text on the Macintosh are proportional spacing, tabs, emphasis, and special characters.

PROPORTIONAL FONTS

The biggest difference between typewriter text and Macintosh text is in the fonts themselves. Figure 4-1 shows some text, first in a typewriter typeface, and then in a standard Macintosh typeface. Immediately you'll notice that each typewriter character is exactly the same width, while the character widths of the Mac font change. This is the difference between *monospaced fonts* and *proportional fonts*.

FIGURE 4-1
Monospaced vs.
Proportional
fonts

```
I aspire to be a legal document someday.
ABCDE abcdefghi 012345
```

I'm happy being nicely typeset. I fit more on a line.
ABCDE abcdefghi 012345

*Each letter is a different
width (proportional)*

*Each letter is exactly the
same width (monospaced)*

This seemingly simple little difference makes a big difference in your typing technique. First of all, if you ever took a typing course like the one I did, you probably had a teacher like mine. Mr. Center always told us to type two spaces after a period or a colon. This is appropriate for a monospaced typewriter face, but is one of the great sins in proportional-font typesetting! You should never type two spaces in a row on the Macintosh (unless perhaps you're in a law office that loves Courier).

Another Mr. Center favorite is the five-space indent. Each paragraph, he said, should begin with five spaces. But I'm on a Mac now, and I know that I should never type two spaces in a row. So the five-space indent is definitely out. Instead, use a first-line indent (see Chapter 5, *Typography*).

TABS

If you've ever used spaces to try and line up a column or two of numbers or words on the Macintosh, you have probably felt a level of frustration unequaled in most other people's lives. It just doesn't work with a proportionally-spaced font. Instead, when you want some text to line up, use a tab (see Figure 4-2).

FIGURE 4-2
Use tabs, not spaces

Sique Cola
"We pay for dentists' summer homes"

Ingredients	percentage	taste factor
Carbonated water	85%	112
Sugar	13%	198
Polyethylene glycol	1%	62

Here, spaces are used to line up these columns

Here, I've used tabs

Ingredients	percentage	taste factor
Carbonated water	85%	112
Sugar	13%	198
Polyethylene glycol	1%	62

Tabs, too, are slightly different on the Macintosh than on a type-writer. The effect is virtually the same (the cursor/carriage moves over to where you placed a tab stop), but word processors on the Macintosh actually insert a tab character in that space. You can go back and adjust the tab stops for that paragraph, or even find and replace the tab characters with something else. Most word processors now have four different types of tabs: left, right, centered and decimal.

If you can avoid it, don't place multiple tabs in a row. That is, if your word processor has default tab stops set at every half-inch, don't type four tabs to get to the 2-inch mark. Just place your own tab stop at that mark and press one tab to get there. This is just another way of simplifying your document so it can be adjusted (tweaked) or modified quickly and painlessly.

EMPHASIS

Remember the days of "tap, tap, tap, tap, backspace, backspace, backspace, backspace, shift-tap, shift-tap, shift-tap, shift-tap" whenever you wanted to underline a word for emphasis? You underlined text for emphasis because that was all you *could* do. Now, however, it's time to move on: use italic or bold styles for emphasis. Don't underline. There are many problems with underlined text, including the inability to precisely position or size the underline (and the line always seems to be the wrong size and in the wrong place). Plus, underlines should never cross a character's descender (the part of a "y," for example, that drops below the baseline), but computers don't pay much attention to this. So don't underline; italicize.

And we shouldn't forget my least favorite way to give emphasis on a typewriter: by typing in all-capital letters. This seems to be one of the hardest habits for some people to break. Do the desktop publishing community (and yourself) a favor: break it. All-capital letters should be used only in extreme emergencies or when typing an acronym. And even in these situations, you should probably use a small-caps style rather than true capital letters (small caps are available in most page-layout programs such as PageMaker and QuarkXPress). The problem is that words set in all caps are more difficult to read. And if there's anything we're trying to do, it's to help, not hinder, the reader.

SPECIAL CHARACTERS

There's one more habit from the "good ol' typewriter days" that we should look at: special characters (see Figure 4-3). You can see all the special characters in a font if you use a desk accessory such as Key Caps or PopChar (or see Tables 4-1 through 4-4).

Em dash. Most good typists have strengthened the pinkies on their right hands for quick and powerful double hyphens. Comments that fall between these double hyphens are like parenthetical remarks: the double hyphen signals a pause in reading. However, on the Macintosh, you should use an em dash (Option-Shift-hyphen).

En dash. The en dash (Option-hyphen), should generally be used for duration and distance, such as in "May–June," "Steps 1–6," and "the San Francisco–Los Angeles trip." It's half as long as an em dash, so it doesn't stand out quite as much.

FIGURE 4-3
Special
characters

So I says to him, "ya' wanna' come to dinna'?" And he replies—get this—"yeah, I do." Ha! Is that a riot or what?

Steve's 34'6"-long boat makes the Bay–Sound run in just under 30 minutes.

Note that the straight single and double quotes here are italic

TABLE 4-1
Special punctua-
tion and symbols
in most fonts

Name	Looks like	Keys to press
Opening double quote	"	Option-[
Closing double quote	"	Option-Shift-[
Opening single quote	'	Option-]
Closing single quote	'	Option-Shift-]
em dash	—	Option-Shift-Hyphen
en dash	–	Option-Hyphen
Ellipsis	…	Option-;
Fraction bar	/	Option-Shift-1
Vertical bar			Shift-\
Capital ligature AE	Æ	Option-Shift-'
Small ligature ae	æ	Option-'
Ligature fi	fi	Option-Shift-5
Ligature fl	fl	Option-Shift-6
Bullet	❺	Option-8
Copyright	©	Option-g
Registered	®	Option-r
Trademark	™	Option-2
Degree	°	Option-Shift-8
Section	§	Option-6
Paragraph	¶	Option-7
Dagger	†	Option-t
Cents	¢	Option-4

Name	Looks like	Keys to press
Left guillemets	«	Option-\
Right guillemets	»	Option-Shift-\
Left single guillemets	‹	Option-Shift-3
Right single guillemets	›	Option-Shift-4
Base double quote	„	Option-Shift-W
Base single quote	‚	Option-Shift-0
Question mark down	¿	Option-Shift-?
Exclamation point down	¡	Option-1
Acute vowel	áéíóúÁÉÍÓÚ	Option-E, then vowel
Umlaut vowel	äëïöüÄËÏÖÜ	Option-U, then vowel
Grave vowel	àèìòùÀÈÌÒÙ	Option-~, then vowel
Circumflex vowel	âêîôûÂÊÎÔÛ	Option-I, then vowel
Cedilla C	Ç	Option-Shift-C
Cedilla c	ç	Option-C
Capital slashed O	Ø	Option-Shift-O
Small slashed o	ø	Option-O
Deutscher double s	ß	Option-S
Dotless i	ı	Option-Shift-B
Tilde	˜	Option-Shift-M
Tilde N	Ñ	Option-N, then Shift-N
Tilde n	ñ	Option-N, then N
Circumflex	ˆ	Option-Shift-N
Macron	ˉ	Option-Shift-,
Breve	˘	Option-Shift-.
Ring accent	°	Option-K
Ring a	å	Option-A
Ring A	Å	Option-Shift-A
Dot accent	·	Option-H
Pound sterling	£	Option-3
Yen	¥	Option-Y

TABLE 4-2 Foreign accents and punctuation

Name	Looks like	Keys to press...
Division	÷	Option-/
Plus or minus	±	Option-Shift-=
Greater or equal	≥	Option-.
Lesser or equal	≤	Option-,
Approximate equal	≈	Option-X

TABLE 4-3 Commonly used math symbols found in most fonts

Not equal	$\neq$	Option-=
Infinity	∞	Option-5
Partial differential	∂	Option-D
Integral	$\int$	Option-B
Florin	f	Option-F
Capital omega	Ω	Option-Z
Capital delta	Δ	Option-J
Product	Π	Option-Shift-P
Summation	Σ	Option-W
Pi	π	Option-P
Radical	$\sqrt{}$	Option-V
Per thousand	‰	Option-Shift-E

TABLE 4-4 Useful Zapf Dingbats characters	**Name**	**Looks like**	**Key to press ...**
	Shadow ballot box up	❏	O
	Shadow ballot box down	❐	P
	3D ballot box up	❑	Q
	3D ballot box down	❒	R
	Filled ballot box	■	N
	Hollow ballot box	□	N (apply outline style)
	Opening big quote	"	Shift-]
	Closing big quote	"	Option-N
	Opening single big quote	'	Shift-[
	Closing single big quote	'	Shift-\
	Great bullet	●	L
	Great hollow bullet	○	L (apply outline style)
	Great shadow bullet	○	M
	Filled arrowhead	➤	Option-Shift-E
	Right arrow	→	Option-]
	Fat right arrow	➡	Option-Shift-U
	3D right arrow	⇨	Option-Shift-I
	Speeding right arrow	➟	Option-Shift-7
	Triangle up	▲	S
	Triangle down	▼	T
	Love leaf	❧	Option-7
	X-mark	✗	8
	Check-mark	✔	4

J'accuse	☞	Shift-=
Victory	✌	Comma
Scissors	✂	Shift-4
Pencil straight	✐	/
Pen nib	✑	1
Telephone	☎	Shift-5
Cross	✚	Shift-;
Star	★	Shift-H
Quatrastar	◆	Shift-F
Octastar	✳	Shift-W
Big asterisk	✸	Shift-Z
Circled sun	✺	B
Snowflake	❄	D

Quotation Marks. The first tip-off that someone in desktop publishing is green behind the ears is his or her use of straight double or single quotes instead of proper "printer's" quotes. Straight quotes, which you get when you press the ' and " keys, should be used for notation of measurements (inches and feet) or for special typographic effects (some fonts' straight quotes look great in headline type). Printer's quotes, also called "curly quotes," should be used for English and American quotations.

Some word processors, such as Microsoft Word, have a feature called "Smart Quotes" which converts straight quotes to curly quotes automatically. I've also included a CDEV called SmartKeys 2 on the Survival Kit disk (see Chapter 11, *Software*) which converts straight quotation marks as you type them.

Nonetheless, I recommend that you get into the habit of typing the odd keystrokes when you need a quote or an apostrophe (Option- and Option-Shift-[and]). Many people create QuicKeys that remap the keyboard so that when they hit a straight quote, they get curly quotes (see Chapter 11, *Software*).

Ligatures. Ligatures are to type what diphthongs are to language. That is, they join characters together. Whereas many classic typefaces would contain 10 ligatures, most typefaces on the Macintosh include only two basic ligatures. Most people don't bother to use them, for some obscure reason. It's a pity, because they really can help a piece of text look great.

The two basic ligatures are the "fi" and the "fl" combinations. They can be typed with the Command-Shift-5 and Command-Shift-6 keystrokes.

Although ligatures make your type look nicer, they may make your life harder. This is because some applications don't presently understand words with ligatures in them. That is, those words come up as "wrong" during a spelling check, they hyphenate improperly, and are difficult to search for. Therefore, it's important to finish all your copyediting tasks first (see "Copyediting," below), then move on to page-formatting tasks like replacing ligatures.

Ellipses. Another form of showing a pause in a conversation or showing a break in quoted text is the ellipsis. Different people type ellipses, sometimes known as "those three dots," in various ways, from "this...and that" (just typing three periods) or "this…and that" (typing the ellipsis character, Option-;) to "this . . . and that" (typing space-period-space-period, and so on). However you type it, you should make sure it's consistent throughout your text (see "House Style Guides," below). Plus, if you use spaces between periods, make sure they're non-breaking spaces (different programs handle these characters differently; consult your software manual).

Registration, copyright, and trademark. The registration, copyright, and trademark symbol characters are found in the Option-R, Option-G, and Option-2 keys, respectively (consult Key Caps or PopChar utilities if you forget). I have only two things to say about using these characters. First, be careful with your sizing and positioning. If your page-layout or word-processing program has the superior-character style, you should probably use that. Otherwise, the symbols appear too large and noticeable.

Second, although you have a legal obligation to print these characters in certain situations, you more often than not don't need to. There are a plethora of lawyers and legal guides out there to help you with these decisions. And, of course, the ultimate decision-making authority on these style questions—as far as I'm concerned—is *The Chicago Manual of Style* (CMOS).

COPYEDITING

The Chicago Manual of Style is a good place to begin this short section on copyediting. CMOS, for many people, is the definitive guide to "how the text should read." That is, what should have an apostrophe, which numbers should be spelled out, how footnotes should read, and so on. The idea is that a sense of consistency not only throughout a single document, but throughout the English language, makes the task of reading somewhat easier for everybody.

Consistency is the key to copyediting. In this section I'm going to throw out a few techniques (such as house style guides and text preparation) and a few suggestions, but ultimately you'll need to develop your own set of guidelines, and methods for following them that suit you.

HOUSE STYLE GUIDES

Open House, a.k.a. Steve and Susie (my dynamic duo editors), has a list of words and phrases that they use to check over manuscripts like mine. For example, if I type "forwards," they'll replace it with "forward," not because of some whim of theirs, but because it fits their house style guide.

Anyone can have a house style guide. It often takes years to build up, and each new project adds to it ("Oh, there's a word that should be on the list"). Meanwhile, many people use other publishers' style guides if they can get their hands on them, or they keep 28 reference books on hand to check every word and phrase.

A house style guide often is customized to the type of text you work with. For example, in our office we write a lot about computers and desktop publishing. Therefore, our house style guide includes lots of words and phrases about computers and desktop publishing.

COPY PROCESSING

It's important to process text to ready it for page layout or final typesetting. This process is called copy preparation (or copy prep, or copy processing). Much of copy prep consists of checking and editing the text so that it conforms to the house style guides and is consistent throughout. Many of these tasks can be performed in a page-layout program, but I much prefer to take care of them in a word-processing program (when you're working with words, it's faster, easier, and more efficient to use a program that focuses on words rather than pages).

A spelling check is a must at this point. It won't catch all your mistakes, though. For example, a spelling checker won't help you avoid embarrassment when you accidently type "pubic transformation" instead of "public transportation" (it's easy to mistype three letters!). So don't forget to proof your copy with an eagle's eye.

When someone else has typed your text, you want to be very careful about checking for double spaces, double hyphens, apostrophes, quotation marks, double spaces between paragraphs, and so on. Here's where search and replace comes in handy. You must also be careful in your use of styles and style sheets (see Chapter 6, *Styles & Codes*).

I've included a checklist of copyediting concerns on the Survival Kit disk that you can customize to your needs.

CHAPTER 5

TYPOGRAPHY

WHAT'S INSIDE

▶ Typography is important because it affects the way that people read the text in your document.

▶ Character formatting—typeface, type size, character style, kerning, and so on—affects only selected text characters.

▶ Paragraph formatting—leading, alignment, indentation, and so on—affects whole paragraphs.

▶ Typographic "color" is the overall gray value created by the optical mixture of black and white in a block of text.

▶ You must be careful of rivers of white space, which often wind their way into justified text.

Back in high-school geometry, I learned that stating one's underlying assumptions (axioms) was essential before going on to discuss the topic at hand. Though geometry won't come into this discussion (are you breathing easier now?), I'll still start out using this method.

Okay. The first axiom in this chapter is: Typography Matters. That means that every little typographic tweak is not made just for fun, but rather is carefully used to further two goals: 1) to make the text readable; and 2) to get a message across.

R. Hunter Middleton (design director emeritus of Ludlow Typograph Company) said, "Typography is the voice of the printed page." Have you ever heard a voice that's so mumbled or scratchy that it's difficult to listen to? What about one where you say, "Wow, I could listen to that for hours."? Figure 5-1 shows you what I mean.

FIGURE 5-1
The voices of typography

Join us for our anniversary cruise through the Thartmond Sound and beyond. We'll follow the whales down the coast, and raise a toast to 25 years of our success.

Sid Vicious does type

Join us for our *anniversary cruise* through the Thartmond Sound and beyond. We'll follow the whales down the coast, and raise a toast to 25 years of our success.

Pavarotti's type

This brings us to the second axiom: Good Typography is Hard Work. Just as a singer has to practice for hours to get a clear tone in her voice, we all have to concentrate to produce good typography. Leaving all the settings in PageMaker or QuarkXPress at their default values won't do it for you.

In this chapter I'm going to discuss most of the elements of typography, if only in passing. This is one area where I'll give you the basics (enough to survive on), but I strongly encourage you to continue this study.

There are two types of typographic controls on the Macintosh: character-based and paragraph-based. The character-based controls let you change the character formatting; the paragraph-based controls let you change the paragraph formatting. It's as easy as that. Let's talk about character formatting first.

CHARACTER FORMATTING

The character-based controls affect only the text characters that you select. If you have selected only one word in a sentence and apply a character style to it, that word (and only that word) is changed.

Character formatting includes typeface, type size, character style, kerning, horizontal scaling, baseline shift, and color. Let's look at each of these control and why you want to think about it.

TYPEFACES

I talked about the technical aspects of fonts and typefaces on the Macintosh back in Chapter 3, *Fonts*. Now, I'll get into their elusive design aspects. Choosing a typeface can be a very personal thing, fraught with implication and the anxiety of decision. Different typefaces are used for different reasons, and there is a time for every typeface under heaven.

In choosing a typeface, you need to be aware of the anatomy of letterforms, including serifs, x-height, ascenders and descenders, and other little tidbits.

Serif, sans serif, and modified sans serif faces. Serifs are those little squiggles or lines that sit at the end of a stroke in some typefaces (see Figure 5-2). The typefaces that have them are called serif fonts; those that don't are called sans serif fonts, and those that are in between are called modified sans serif fonts.

▶ *Serif.* There are various theories about where serif faces first came from, but the important thing to remember is that large blocks of text are usually easier to read when set in serif faces. For example, the body copy of this book is set in Utopia. Other examples of serif typefaces include Times, Palatino, Gara-mond, and Cheltenham. Some people call these roman faces.

FIGURE 5-2
Serif, sans serif,
and modified
sans serif
typefaces

Very Swiss, you know. *Helvetica*

Do you know me? I'm Omar Seríf. *Times*

The new Opti-grab typeface! *Optima*

▶ ***Sans serif.*** If a typeface doesn't have serifs, it's called a sans serif (French for "without serif") typeface. Sans serif type first appeared about 170 years ago, but really became popular during this century. These faces are often associated with Futurist or Bauhaus designs of the 1920s and 1930s, and are often called grotesque, Swiss, or gothic typefaces.

While serif faces are often used for the main text, sans s faces are excellent for headlines, for section heads, and for other smaller blocks of text. Some examples of sans serif typefaces are Helvetica, Futura, and Univers.

▶ ***Modified sans serif.*** As with any other form of classification, there are always those items that don't fall into any particular category. For example, the typeface Optima really isn't a serif or a sans serif. It's sort of like a tomato, which is both fruit and vegetable. Optima, at first glance, seems to be a sans serif face, but it has slight swellings at the ends of its horizontal and vertical strokes which give it an effect similar to traditional serif typefaces.

X-height. The x-height of a typeface (the height of a lowercase "x" in that face) is the second most important feature you should consider. The measurement of the x-height is not as important as its size in proportion to the height of the capital letters. For example, Adobe Garamond has proportionally a much smaller x-height than Helvetica (see Figure 5-3). Typefaces with proportionally larger x-heights often give an impression of stability and robustness.

Ascenders and descenders. The letters g, d, y, k, and q all have something in common: they either ascend above the x-line or

FIGURE 5-3
X-height

Now showing! X-height wars! Featuring:

Spectrum *versus* **Helvetica**

descend below the baseline. The parts of the letterform that ascend or descend are called ascenders or descenders. Ascenders usually are the same height as capital letters, though they occasionally are even taller.

Other tidbits. When looking at typefaces, you should also notice such elements as counters (for example, the open spaces inside the "o" and "a"), stroke width contrast, and character width. For example, ITC Garamond always seems too wide to me; the lowercase "o" is almost extended. On the other hand, Adobe Garamond (which is almost a totally different face) has a much more reasonable "o."

Each of these elements changes the typeface, and the way readers feel about what they're reading. When choosing a typeface, you must ask yourself, "Does this face convey what I'm trying to say?"

TYPE SIZE

I don't care what people say: size *does* matter. Type is traditionally measured in points (½ inch), but 24-point type is rarely 24 points high. Originally, "24-point" referred to the size of the type's metal body (from a bit below the lowest descender, to a bit above the tallest ascender). However, with digital type, you can't even be assured of that. Therefore (as we'll see repeatedly throughout this chapter), you need to use your eyes, and make a decision about how large your type should be.

For example, you might design a newsletter using 10-point Palatino, and it'll be very legible. However, if you changed the face to 10-point Monotype Spectrum, the text might be difficult for some people over forty to read. Monotype Spectrum has a much smaller x-height, and very fine stroke widths. Therefore it appears smaller (see Figure 5-4).

Remember, too, that even tiny changes in point size can make a significant difference in appearance. You may not see it on your

FIGURE 5-4
Type sizes aren't
always what
you'd think

Go, charge my goblins that they grind their joints
With dry convulsions, shorten up their sinews
With aged cramps, and more pinch-spotted make them
Than pard or cat o'mountain.

Go, charge my goblins that
they grind their joints
With dry convulsions, shorten
up their sinews
With aged cramps, and more
pinch-spotted make them
Than pard or cat o'mountain.

Both of these are 10-point
type with 13-point leading

desktop laser printer, but if you print to an imagesetter, a half point can make all the difference.

CHARACTER STYLES

When the Macintosh first came out, I must admit I created some of the worst-looking type ever. Just because I could, I set single words in bold, outline, and shadow, then—as if that wasn't enough—I underlined them, for emphasis. There's nothing wrong with playing around like this; it's fun. But I hope you don't do it on a client's job!

Different programs let you set text in different character styles, but they almost all allow for roman, italic, bold, outline, shadow, strikethrough, small capitals, and underline. Figure 5-5 shows examples of these styles, plus several more for the sake of reference.

The primary use of these styles is for emphasis. However, in professional typesetting, the only styles you should use are italic, bold, and small caps. Of course, it's easy to find exceptions to this rule. The other styles can be useful in the course of developing the copy. For example, my editor uses strikethrough to suggest deletions, and underline to suggest additions. However, underlining in a finished document just shows that you haven't adjusted from the typewriter days when you couldn't make text italic (see "Emphasis" in Chapter 4, *Word Processing*).

Once again, you should use a style when and where necessary to give a particular effect (see Figure 5-6).

KERNING AND TRACKING

Kerning is the addition or removal of space between two characters. Tracking, often called range kerning, is the adjustment of space between all the characters in a group of text. Kerning and tracking are two subtle yet powerful tools for achieving clean, easy-to-read typography. And, conversely, bad kerning and tracking stand out like a scared armadillo on a Texas roadside (see Figure 5-7).

FIGURE 5-5
Character styles

Plain text

Boldface

Italics

Outline

Shadow

~~Strike-through~~

<u>Underlined (everything)</u>

<u>Word</u> <u>underlining</u>

LARGE & SMALL CAPS

ALL CAPS

Su^{per}script (*baseline shown as dotted line*)

Sub$_{script}$

Superior char^{acters}

FIGURE 5-6
Use these styles
sparingly

The Fastest Racing Sailboat Under 14 Feet!

Pessimist

Only $899^{95}

See it in our showrooms, open from 9 AM to 5 PM,

Monday–Saturday

6993 Marcel Drive

"Right down by the water"

*Small caps, superior, and underline
attributes are great if used in
moderation and in the right places.*

FIGURE 5-7
Kerning and tracking

AVATAR   *Unkerned*

AVATAR   *With automatic kerning*

AVATAR   *Tight manual kerning*

Prospero   *Tight tracking (range kerning)*

Prospero   *Normal tracking*

Prospero   *Loose tracking*

Most fonts have a number of kerning pairs (preset kerning values for two characters, such as "To" or "Aw") built into them. However, some programs—like Microsoft Word—don't pay any attention to these preset values (and won't let you kern pairs manually, either). This is the biggest typographic difference between page layout programs and word processing programs: word processors don't need great-looking text. Designers do.

In applications that do include kerning and tracking controls, you must generally either work in points or in fractions of an em space. An em is (unfortunately) defined differently in different programs, but is a value usually approximately equivalent to the size of the type. That is, any 24-point type would have a 24-point em space, and a kerning value of $\frac{1}{10}$ of that em would equal 2.4 points. What's important here is that if you're adjusting kerning in fractions of an em, if or when you change the size of the type, the kerning changes, too. It's proportional to the type size, rather than a fixed amount of space.

Here are a couple of quick rules for kerning and tracking.

▶ Text in all capital letters usually needs a little space added overall.

▶ Printing white text on a black background often requires a little looser tracking, too.

▶ Larger type needs to be tracked tighter (using negative tracking values). Often, the larger the type, the tighter it should be, though there are aesthetic exceptions to this rule. Advertising headlines will often be tracked until the characters just "kiss."

▶ Condensed typefaces, such as Futura Condensed, can usually do with a hair tighter tracking.

Remember, however, that no matter how solid a rule, you are obliged to break it if the finished design will be the better for it.

HORIZONTAL SCALING

Imagine the characters in a typeface as being rubber and stretchable. Now imagine stretching a typeface, that took hundreds of hours to laboriously design at a specific width, to 60 percent of its size, distorting the characters into forms they were never meant to be. Now imagine the type designer's face.

Okay, you get the idea: typefaces were designed to be specific widths, and they shouldn't be messed with unless you have some really good reasons. What are some good reasons? The best reason of all is that you really want the typeface to look that way. But compressing Helvetica to 70 percent just because you don't feel like buying a true Helvetica Condensed from Adobe is a pretty cruddy reason (see Figure 5-7).

FIGURE 5-7
Horizontal
scaling

You want to give this dude
a WIDE berth,
cuz he's, like, extremely
narrow-minded

Another good reason to play with the horizontal scaling is if you need to make some body copy fit a particular space. Here I'm talking about changing the horizontal scaling 2 or 3 percent, not 10 or 20 percent. Almost no one can see this small of an adjustment.

BASELINE SHIFT

When you talk about "a line of text," you generally are indirectly referring to the baseline that all the characters "sit" on. Many programs now let you move individual characters vertically up or down from this baseline, creating what is called baseline shift. This is particularly helpful for typesetting equations and fractions, and for adding symbols such as the registered trademark characters (see Figure 5-8).

FIGURE 5-8
Baseline shift

$$\frac{9}{8} \quad \text{BASELINE SHIFT}$$

$$E=MC^2$$

COLOR AND TINT

Coloring or tinting text isn't really a typographic feature, but so many programs now allow this as a character-level attribute that I thought I'd throw it in anyway. A note on the subject: printing a color or a tint value on a black-and-white printer (and many color printers, too) results in the color being simulated by dots (see Chapter 7, *Scans & Halftones*). Usually the eye blends the dots together, so that they seem like a solid color or gray value. However, fine serifs or counters in small type often get fuzzy or clogged and look odd when represented this way (see Figure 5-9). I'm not saying not to tint or color type. I'm just saying that you need to be careful when doing so.

FIGURE 5-9
Tinted type

Miranda and Caliban

Miranda and Caliban

PARAGRAPH FORMATTING

Now let's move on to paragraph formatting. These are attributes that control entire paragraphs of text. Let me be clear about this: a paragraph is any block of text that ends with a carriage return (the "Return" key). This could be one word, or one sentence, or several sentences. I know it sounds simple, but many people get messed up with this.

Paragraph formatting includes leading, alignment, indentation, space before and after, and widow and orphan control. Let's look at each of these and why they're important.

LEADING

Leading (pronounced "ledding") is the space between lines of type. The name originates from the strips of lead that were placed between lines of metal type. Most Macintosh applications give you considerable control over leading values for each paragraph, but they also let you set leading to automatic. "Automatic" can mean any number of things, depending on the application, but I define it as "whatever-you-do-don't-use-me." Why? Because it's a default value, and following the defaults is like a sheep following a blind shepherd.

I usually set a text block's leading to about 120 percent of its size. That is, 10-point type is set with 12 points of leading. This is called "10 on 12" and is often represented as "10/12." However, this is a rule just waiting to be broken. Here's a list of some more leading "rules."

▶ Increase the leading as you increase the line length. Solid leading (for example, 12 on 12) may read fine with lines containing five words, but will be awful for lines containing 20 words.

▶ Generally use some extra leading for sans serif or bold type. It needs the extra space.

▶ Note the x-height of the typeface. Faces with small x-heights can often be set more tightly than those with large x-heights.

▶ Consider setting display or headline type tightly. Large type can be set tightly, using either solid leading or leading less than the point size of the type.

▶ When you're using really tight leading, be careful not to let the ascenders of one line touch the descenders of the line above it.

Once again, I encourage you to break the rules if you have a good reason for doing so.

Because so many people use Aldus PageMaker, I should note here that leading in that program is handled as a character-level attribute, rather than a paragraph-level attribute. My officemate Olav Kvern and I argue over whether this makes sense or not. I don't think so; he does (he almost always wins that debate).

HORIZONTAL ALIGNMENT

If you've been involved with desktop typography long enough (a day or two), you'll know that different applications have different names for the same thing. For example, what QuarkXPress calls "left-aligned," just about every other program calls "left-justified," "flush left," or "ragged right." I happen to like the way Quark does it, so that's the word I'll use: aligned.

Figure 5-10 is worth a thousand words in trying to describe what horizontal alignment is all about. I have just a couple of things to say about it.

FIGURE 5-10
Horizontal
alignment

They ain't bothering about faith. They lost their farm.	*Left-aligned*
They're no Protestants. They're Catholics like us.	*Center-aligned*
No way of sorting 'em out in a bombardment.	*Right-aligned*

I know you would never do this. I know you're a designer of reputation and flair. But I might as well mention this, just in case: Don't use left-aligned, right-aligned, centered and justified text all on the same page, unless you have good design sense and a signed note from your parent. Too often, people let all this highfalutin' technology go to their heads, and design their pages using every trick in the book. Remember that there is strength in subtlety.

The second thing I need to mention regards centered text. The computer only thinks in numbers, and you need to remember that the mathematical centering of text may not look as correct as optical centering, especially if you have punctuation before or after the text. You can use invisible characters (colored white) or altered indention to change the position of the text (see Figure 5-11). Just remember that what looks right is more "right" than what the computer says.

FIGURE 5-11
Centering text

"Take your little brother swimming with a brick."

Mathematically centered

"Take your little brother swimming with a brick."

Optically centered

INDENTATION

A paragraph's indentation is determined by where its left and right margins are, and what its first-line indent is set to. Let's take a quick look at each of these.

Margins. Different programs have very different ways of specifying the default margins of a block of text. Aldus PageMaker sets them at the width of the text block. Microsoft Word has these values set in the Document dialog box. Whatever the case, you can usually change both the left and right margins on a paragraph level by using Left Indent and Right Indent. Some programs let you specify both positive and negative values (moving the margin in or out), and others just allow positive values (nesting that paragraph in from both sides).

First-line indent. Whatever you do, wherever you go, don't type five spaces to indent the first line of each paragraph. Instead, use a first-line indent, which indents only the first line of the paragraph.

How deep your indent should be depends primarily on your design and on the typeface you are using. If you are using a typeface with a large x-height, you should specify a larger first line-indent than if you are working with a small x-height font.

Hanging indents. You can use left indents and first-line indents to create hanging indents, which are used for lists with bullets, and the like. You do this by typing a positive left indent and a negative first-line indent. For example, I often use 1p6 (one pica, six points) for a left indent and –1p6 for a first-line indent. This places the first character of the paragraph (a bullet) at the zero mark, and the subsequent lines at the 1p6 mark (see Figure 5-12). In most programs, typing a tab after the bullet character jumps the cursor over to the 1p6 mark, whether or not there's really a tab stop there.

FIGURE 5-12
Hanging indents

• Hey! No way am I going to hang out with that stupid bullet over there.

Left indent: 2 picas
First-line indent: –2 picas

SPACE BEFORE AND SPACE AFTER

Let me see if I can be as clear as when I wrote "Don't use multiple spaces between words or punctuation." Don't ever use an extra carriage return to add space between paragraphs. If you do, nine times out of ten you will mess yourself up with extra blank paragraphs hanging out at tops of columns or in other places where you don't want them. Instead, use the Space Before or Space After settings in your program.

These settings control the amount of extra space between each paragraph. Usually they're set to zero, but you can add space before or after a paragraph by changing the settings. Space Before usually doesn't affect the first paragraph in a text block (or at the top of a page), but it might (it does in MS Word), so be careful. Also, I usually just use one or the other of these settings in a document. That is, if I want a .125-inch space between each paragraph, I set either Space Before or Space After to this value (usually Space Before). The only time I set both values for a paragraph is when I'm setting heads or subheads. For example, a subhead might have 12 points before it and 4 points after it.

WIDOW AND ORPHAN CONTROL

I mean no disrespect to widows and orphans, but when it comes to typesetting, we must carefully control them, stamping out their very existence when we have the chance.

If you know what I'm talking about already, bear with me or skip this paragraph (or test whether you can remember which is the widow and which is the orphan). A widow is the last line of a paragraph that winds up all by itself at the top of a column or page. An orphan is the first line of a paragraph that sits all by itself at the bottom of a column or page. I like to use the following mnemonic device: widows sounds like "windows," which are high up (top of the page), whereas orphans make me think of tiny Oliver (who was small, and thus at the bottom of the page).

Typesetters sometimes also refer to a line of text comprised of only one word as either a widow or an orphan. To avoid the confusion, in our office we prefer the word "runt."

All typographic widows and orphans are bad, but certain kinds are really bad—for example, a line that consists of only one word, or even the last part of a hyphenated word. Another related typographic horror is the subhead that stands alone with its following paragraph on the next page.

Fortunately, there are ways to avoid such typographic travesties. Subtle horizontal scaling, sizing, or tracking can work to pull or push type around. Many programs now include Keep with Next Paragraph or Keep Paragraph Together features (ensuring that important paragraphs and subheads stay together). My last resort—but often the most effective one—is simply to rewrite the paragraph (unless it's not my business to do so).

TIPS AND TECHNIQUES

Let's remind ourselves of the initial axioms of this chapter: Typography Matters, and: Good Typography is Hard Work. In this chapter we've looked at the major tools of desktop typography: character and paragraph formatting. However, much of what is difficult about creating good typography is looking at the big picture: how does the paragraph, page, chapter, or book look? Before we move on, I want to throw out three more concepts for you to work with: color, rivers, and page grids.

WHEN BLACK AND WHITE IS COLORFUL

When designers and typesetters talk about the color of a page or the color of type, they probably aren't talking red, green, or blue. They're referring to the degree of darkness or lightness that the text projects. The color of text is directly related to the typeface, the letter spacing, word spacing, and leading. You can talk about the color of word, a line of type, a paragraph, or even a whole page. It's usually good practice to maintain an even and balanced color, unless you're trying to pull the viewer's eye to one area or another (see Figure 5-13).

FIGURE 5-13
The color, or gray value, of type

The sea is calm tonight the moon lies fair upon the straits. On the French coast the light gleams and is gone. Come to the window. Sweet is the night air. Only, from the sea-blanched sand where the see meets the shingle. The sea is calm tonight the moon lies fair upon the straits.

The sea is calm tonight the moon lies fair upon the straits. On the French coast the light gleams and is gone. Come to the window. Sweet is the night air. Only, from the sea-blanched sand where the see meets the shingle.

The sea is calm tonight the moon lies fair upon the straits. On the French coast the light gleams and is gone. Come to the window. Sweet is the night air. Only, from the sea-blanched sand where the see meets the shingle. The sea is calm

RIVERS

Often the first problem that arises when people set their text in justified alignment is that their documents start looking like a flood just hit; rivers of space flow down the page around little islands of words. Too much space between words is disturbing to the eye.

One of the best ways to check for both the color of a page and for rivers is to hold the printed page backwards up to the light, so you can see the text blocks without being distracted by the text itself. Some people can do the same thing by holding the page at a distance (right side up) and squinting severely, or by holding it upside down.

It's easier to find a river than to make it disappear. The main tools at your disposal are hyphenation and justification controls, manually hyphenating words, changing the tracking, and rewriting the text (if it's yours to rewrite!).

PAGE GRIDS

There are already enough books about good design. However, I will bring up one element of quality page design that relates to typography: page grids. A page grid is an invisible grid structure to which everything on a page aligns: text blocks, rules, pictures, and so on. This means that the tops (and bottoms, as much as possible) of text blocks should vertically align to this grid (see Figure 5-14).

One subtle but very important ramification of the page grid concept is that each line of text on a page should line up with the text in adjacent columns (see Figure 5-15). As I said earlier, these principles aren't applied just for fun: they ensure that your audience

FIGURE 5-14
Align
blocks of
text vertically

Be not afeard; the isle is full of noises, sounds, and sweet airs, that give delight and hurt not. Sometimes a thousand twangling instruments will hum about mine ears; and sometime voices that, if I then had waked after long sleep, will make me sleep again; and then, in dreaming, the clouds

methought would open, and show riches ready upon me, that when I waked I cried to dream again. Be not afeard; the isle is full of noises, sounds, and sweet airs, that give delight and hurt not. Sometimes a thousand twangling instruments will hum about mine ears; and

sometime voices that, if I then had waked after long sleep, will make me sleep again; and then, in dreaming, the clouds methought would open, and show riches ready upon me, that when I waked I cried to dream again.Be not afeard; the isle is full of noises, sounds, and sweet airs, that give

The baselines of these columns should all align

can read your page easily and efficiently. At the same time, there are times when you either will not want to, or cannot, follow them. As always, use your best design judgment.

FIGURE 5-15
Align lines of text
across a page

and I will be happy to do whatever you please.

Signora Emilia:
Signor Unico, God save me even from thinking, much less doing, anything to cause you to be hated; for

not only would I be doing what I ought not, but I should be thought to show little judgement in attempting the impossible. But since you urge me thus to speak of what pleases

The lines in these columns do not align.

and I will be happy to do whatever you please.

Signora Emilia:
Signor Unico, God save me even from thinking, much less doing, anything to

cause you to be hated; for not only would I be doing what I ought not, but I should be thought to show little judgement in attempting the impossible. But since you urge me thus

These lines do.

STYLES & CODES

WHAT'S INSIDE

▶ A paragraph style is a collection of character and paragraph formatting information that has a name.

▶ You can apply local character and paragraph formatting that override paragraph styles.

▶ Various programs let you create, apply and manipulate paragraph styles differently.

▶ Although WYSIWYG screen displays make most formatting tasks easy, sometimes it's appropriate to use programming or typesetting codes.

I always thought you had to work hard to be successful in business. But no longer. Now I'm a convert to the lazy person's ethic: be effective while doing as little work as possible.

The computer is designed to make life easier for you, so why not let it? In this chapter we're going to look over the various methods for letting the computer do all the boring, methodical work for you so that you can have more time to sharpen your skills as a sailor, skiier or professional couch-potato. The primary areas that we'll look at are style sheets, style tags, and code-based typesetting.

STYLE SHEETS

If you never make mistakes, then you can skip this section. Otherwise, stay tuned for some hot tips for success.

The biggest secret to smart desktop publishing is saving your work often and making backup files. The second biggest secret is using paragraph styles. Paragraph styles are different from paragraph formatting (see Chapter 5, *Typography*), but they're not any more difficult to work with. A paragraph style, which is usually just called "style," is simply a collection of formatting information that has a name. For example, you can make a style called "First Paragraph" that is defined as Helvetica Bold 11/13, no first-line indent, with six points of space before the paragraph. All the text in any paragraph that is assigned (or tagged with) this style name will be formatted to these specifications.

The concept I want to get across here is that paragraph (and character) styles are very different from formatting. A style gives something (like a paragraph) a name. Formatting specifies what that thing *looks like*. When you apply a paragraph style, you're tagging it with a style name. That name can be linked with a collection of formatting, but is not the formatting itself.

A style sheet is the list of all the paragraph styles in a document (you can think of this as a sheet of paper with all the styles listed).

Before I go any further, I should clarify one point: just about everyone uses the terminology I'm talking about here. However, QuarkXPress doesn't. QuarkXPress uses the phrase "style sheet" for both the styles and the list of styles. I don't know why, and it doesn't matter much. With that said, let's go on with the discussion.

LOCAL FORMATTING

Before I knew enough to use styles, I used local formatting. Local formatting is any character and/or paragraph formatting that you apply directly to your text. For example, if I wanted a paragraph to be set in Times Roman, I'd select the whole paragraph and apply that font to it. Likewise, if I wanted that paragraph to have 12-point leading, I would apply that leading directly to the paragraph. Formatting an entire magazine was no fun: I'd spend an hour making sure each subhead was correctly formatted, then I'd spend another two hours working on the body text. When my client decided (at 4:30 on Friday afternoon) to change the typeface of all the subheads and the leading of all the body text, I didn't know whether to kill myself or him!

There's a technical word for this method of formatting: *stupid*.

WORKING SMART WITH STYLES

The smart way to format a document is to take the time to be lazy. Create a paragraph style for each type of paragraph in your document, and apply those styles to each paragraph of your text. I won't lie to you: it does take a little longer to set up your document, but if you have any more than one page of text, I assure you that you'll save time in the long run.

For example, let's say you're creating a newsletter. You know that you've got body text, masthead text, and two levels of headings. Right at the beginning of your formatting, create a style for each one of these elements. You don't even need to have the design exactly the way you want it. Then go through and apply a style to every paragraph (e.g., "BodyText" to your body copy, "AHead" to your first-level heads, and so on). This takes a little concentration (you don't want to leave a paragraph out). As you apply the styles, each paragraph's character and paragraph formatting changes quickly.

If any part of the type design changes (like typeface, leading, horizontal scaling, and so on), you can use the style controls in your program to alter that style. When you press OK, every paragraph that was assigned (tagged with) that style changes.

CREATING STYLES

Different programs have different ways of creating and modifying styles, so check your user's manual. However, most applications let you create a style that includes almost every character- and paragraph-formatting feature available in that program.

One style sheet feature that most applications have is the "Based On" control. This lets you base one paragraph style on another. For example, in the newsletter scenario above, you might want the masthead text to be exactly the same as the body text, except two points smaller and with no first-line indent. You can create the "Masthead" style (or name it whatever you like) by first basing it on the "BodyText" style, and then making adjustments to that style. In Microsoft Word, you get a style description that looks something like this: "BodyText + Font: 10 pt, First Indent: 0."

Basing one style on another can allow you to quickly change much of the text in a document through a domino effect. For example, if all text blocks are based on a style named Text and all the heads are based on a style called Heads, then all you have to do is change two styles, and the entire document changes.

APPLYING STYLES

Remember that when you apply a paragraph style, the formatting is applied to an entire paragraph, not just to the text that you have selected (see "Character Styles," below). You can, however, override a paragraph's style with local formatting. For example, if you want a single word to be in italic, you would select it and make it italic. Note that this is different than the "stupid" local formatting I talked about earlier. If you're formatting your whole document (or even a whole paragraph) with local formatting, you're probably making life difficult for yourself. But if you need to give emphasis to a word, then you must use local character formatting (unless your software has character styles).

Tagged text. Different software programs let you tag paragraphs with styles by using various methods. For example, PageMaker, Ventura Publisher, and QuarkXPress have palettes that display the style sheet for that document. You can simply select the paragraph(s) to be tagged, then click on the style in the palette.

There is another way to apply paragraph styles to text, though: pretagging. Pretagging involves coding ASCII text with special comments that tag each paragraph with a style (see "Codes," below). For example, when a paragraph preceded by the tag "<Normal>" is imported into PageMaker, that paragraph comes in tagged as the Normal style. Again, various programs handle pretagging differently.

IMPORTING AND EXPORTING STYLES

Most programs let you save, import and export text with its paragraph styles attached. This is helpful when moving text from one program to another. For example, this book was written entirely in Microsoft Word. While I wrote, I applied a style to each paragraph (or I let Word apply it for me automatically). When the text was imported into QuarkXPress, the paragraph styles came with it.

The way that programs handle importing and exporting text with paragraph styles varies. However, in most programs, when you import tagged text into a document that has same-named styles, the paragraph style description in the document overrides the incoming style description. Again, looking at this book as an example, the body text in Microsoft Word was set in a style named BodyText, which was specified as 12-point Palatino. The QuarkXPress templates also had a style called BodyText, but this one was set to 9.5-point Utopia (which is what you're reading). When we imported the Word documents, the paragraphs retained the paragraph style name BodyText, but the character and paragraph formatting changed into QuarkXPress style descriptions.

CODES

Let's just take a quick trip down memory lane. In the "olden days" (about six years ago), almost all typesetting was done on code-based text composition machines. A compositor (someone who had to sit at these machines) would usually type all the text into the machine, inserting a number of codes into the text, such as <LS12><FT121> <LL22> <PS12>A<PS6><BU6><PS12>Y, which sets an A and a Y next to each other, with a gnat's whisker of kerning between. When the compositor wanted to see what the page would really look like, she would either flip into preview mode or print the page out. This is how many PC programs still handle text formatting.

The introduction of WYSIWYG (What You See Is What You Get) on Macintosh screens let these compositors (and you) actually format characters and paragraphs, as well as apply paragraph and character styles, directly on the "preview" page itself. However, this user interface had (and has) its down side. It turns out that there are some very powerful text-processing controls that are available only with code-based systems. Fortunately, many programs on the Mac are now letting you meld the best of both worlds together (see Figure 6-1).

FIGURE 6-1
XPress Tags
combine codes
and tags

Gadzooks! Zounds! Eeep! How such a simple mistake could snowball into the *catastrophe* this has become. No longer am I in control of my destiny. Kismet has come and swept my porch too, too

@Normal=<*L*h"Standard"*kn0*kt0*ra0*rb 0*d0*p(0,0,0,0,0,0,g)*t(0,0," "): Ps100t0h100z12k0b0c"Black"f"Helvetica"> Ps100t0h100z10k0b0c"Black"f"Avant Garde">Gadzooks! Zounds! <t-1>Eeep! How such a<t0> simple mis<\h>take could snowball into the <I>catastrophe <I>this has become. No longer am I in control of my destiny. Kismet has come and swept my porch too, too clean. Oh, weary day.

The page looks like this   *The codes look like this*

For example, Mike Arst (who does Macintosh code work better than anyone I know) can export text from QuarkXPress, search for all words that are longer than two letters and are set in all caps, then change them to small caps. Finally, he'll import the text back into QuarkXPress to complete his layout. When he's producing a technical book, he can use this to quickly change all those techie words like DOS, EPSF, and RTFM into small caps (the way they often should be in typeset materials).

CHAPTER 7

SCANS & HALFTONES

WHAT'S INSIDE

▶ Bitmapped images usually come from either scanners or paint programs. Scanners create scans; paint programs create synthetic bitmapped images.

▶ Scanners fall into one of several categories: reflective art scanners, transparent art scanners, or video capture scanners.

▶ "Scanning smart" means looking ahead and asking yourself all the right questions.

▶ You often need to process scans with programs like Adobe Photoshop.

▶ Halftones are necessary to print gray tints on black-and-white printers.

▶ Halftone cells are built from dots. The cells are arranged at a specified angle and screen frequency.

▶ Computers only know that bitmapped images are a series of dots. If you have a scan of text, you must process it with OCR software before you can manipulate the text with a word processor.

I know that you're not the type of person to do something like this, but I know a guy who tried to use a word processor to read a gray-scale image scan of a page of text. I'll tell you right now that it didn't work. He was not a stupid man. It's just that he fell prey to a common assumption that the Macintosh computer seamlessly brings together all the elements of desktop publishing (scans, text, illustrations, and so on) without his having to think about a thing.

In this chapter, we're going to look at scans and other bitmapped images. We touched on this area briefly back in Chapter 2, *Graphic File Formats*, but it's worth going over in more depth. Later in the chapter, I'll cover halftones and optical character recognition (OCR).

BITMAPPED IMAGES

If you're like me, you just don't have time to look back at Chapter 2, *Graphic File Formats*, to refresh your memory of bitmapped images and the PNTG and TIFF file types. So, here are the highlights.

▶ Bitmapped images are simply rectangular grids of pixels (dots).

▶ The image resolution is the number of these dots per inch (or per centimeter).

▶ Each pixel is assigned to be black, white, a level of gray, or a color. This color is represented by a number; for example, black might be 256 in a 256-gray-level file.

▶ Scaling the image has a direct effect on its resolution. Enlarging the picture 200 percent cuts the resolution in half, which may result in jaggies or pixelation. Reducing the image 50 percent doubles the resolution, which may improve image quality.

▶ A PNTG (Paint-type) file has fixed dimensions of 8 by 10 inches at 72 dots per inch—that's 576 by 720 pixels—and each pixel can be either white or black. These are said to be "flat" or bilevel bitmapped images.

> A TIFF file can be any size rectangle with any number of dots per inch, and each pixel can have any level of gray or color. TIFF files are said to be "deep" if they contain four or more gray levels (more than 2 bits per sample point).

> PICT files can contain bitmapped images; however, PICT files are unreliable.

THE ORIGINS OF BITMAPPED IMAGES

Okay. So we know about these things called bitmapped images. How do we actually get one? Bitmapped images usually come from two sources: either from a scanner (which produces scans), or from a software paint program (which produces synthetic bitmaps). Let's look at each of these.

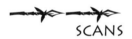

SCANS

The function of a scanner is to get an image from the real world into the computer. An image you've scanned using the methods outlined below is saved on disk as a bitmapped image of one type or another. Neither the computer nor the scanner knows what the image is. It could be text, or it could be a photograph, or it could be a line drawing. This is an important concept to get. The computer only knows that it's a bunch of dots.

Although scanners can look drastically different, there are really only three basic types: reflective art scanners, transparent art scanners, and video capture scanners. Let's look at each of these.

Reflective art. This is the type of scanner that you're probably most familiar with. It may be a flatbed scanner (on which you can lay a book or a photograph), a roll-feed scanner (which only takes flat sheets of paper), a drum scanner (this also only takes flat sheets), or even a handheld type (which you manually move over an image). It works by flashing a very bright light on the page and reading how much light is reflected back from a very small point (often measuring 1/300 inch). This is called "sampling." It repeats this process for every point on the page.

All reflective art scanners can generally scan at between 288 and 600 dpi, and "see" between 16 and 256 levels of gray. For example, the ThunderScan scanner is a 288-dpi 5-bit scanner, which means it can see 288 dots per inch, and each of these dots is one of 32 levels of gray (including black and white). Here in my office, we use an HP ScanJet Plus, which is a 300-dpi 8-bit scanner: it sees 256 levels of gray at 300 dots per inch. The ScanJet Plus (as well as other scanners) can use mathematical algorithms to interpolate dots in between the actual sample points, simulating more than 300 dots per inch.

Transparent art. If you are trying to scan a 35mm slide or a 4-by-5-inch transparency, you'll want to use a scanner that can accommodate transparent art. Such a scanner uses the same process as a reflective art scanner, except that it measures or samples light shining through the art rather than reflecting from it. Many reflective art scanners have attachments for transparent art. You can generally get a better scan from a transparent art scanner for two reasons. First, the light that bounces off your artwork in a reflective art scanner changes, depending on the artwork. That is, you can get a different scan (one perhaps better than the other) from the same picture, depending on whether it's on coated or uncoated paper.

Second, because transparent art scanners usually are looking at small 35mm slides, they need to have a very high scanning resolution. For example, the Nikon LS-3500 can scan at 4,096 dots per inch. Because the image is scanned at such a high resolution, when the image is enlarged to the size you want, the loss of resolution probably won't affect the image quality.

Video capture. You can also capture still images from a videotape or from a digital video camera, using specialized software and hardware. Video images are almost always 24 bit, at either 640 by 480 pixels (for NTSC in America) or 768 by 576 pixels (for PAL in Europe). When you first capture them, they usually appear at 72 dpi (depending on the software you're using). Therefore, to achieve a reasonable resolution for printing, you must often scale these images down to 20 or 30 percent of their original size (more on this topic later in the chapter).

SYNTHETIC BITMAPPED IMAGES

Instead of creating bitmapped images with a scanner, you can create your own bitmapped images (synthetic bitmapped images) using a paint program such as Adobe Photoshop, Oasis, or Letraset's ColorStudio. Each of these programs lets you create an image from scratch or start with another bitmapped image (even a scan) and modify it (see Figure 7-1). Synthetic bitmapped images also come from screen captures (snapshots of your computer screen).

FIGURE 7-1
Synthetic
bitmapped
images from a
paint program

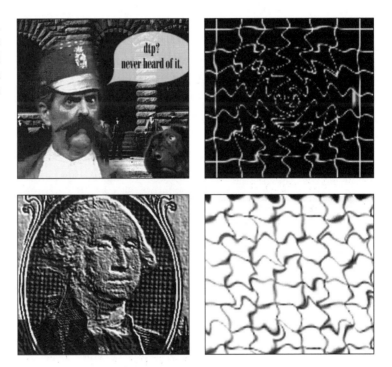

SCANNING SMART

When my friend Greg Vander Houwen creates a scan or a synthetic bitmapped image for publication, he doesn't work at the highest resolution he can. He works at the highest resolution he needs to. I call this the difference between scanning smart and scanning stupid. Scanning stupid is taking a 2-by-2-inch black-and-white line drawing and scanning it as a 300-dpi 8-by-10-inch image at 8 bits (256 levels of gray), then printing it at 50 percent of size on an ImageWriter. Your scanned file is going to be 7,078K, and will take 20 times longer to print out than if you scanned smart.

Scanning smart is looking ahead and asking yourself the right questions. Here's a sampling of some questions to ask.

▶ What kind of printer will this image be printed on?

▶ What is that printer's resolution?

▶ How many levels of gray can that printer produce?

▶ What kind of artwork am I scanning (or creating)? One-bit? Eight-bit? Twenty-four-bit?

▶ If printing a halftone image, what screen frequency will I print at? (See "Halftones," later in this chapter.)

In the example given above, scanning smart would dictate that you only scan the 2-by-2-inch area as a flat (1-bit) 200-dpi image. When you reduced the image 50 percent, you would get a 400-dpi image, which is probably good enough. This file is 20K (and will take approximately .3 percent of the time to print, import, or manipulate).

Here's the formula for figuring the size of a scan: width (in inches) × height (in inches) × resolution^2 (in dots per inch) × bits per sample ÷ 8,192 = kilobytes. (8,192 is the number of bits in a kilobyte.)

POST-PROCESSING SCANS

Scans, like the computer that produces them, are only as good as the person who's working with them. There are two problems with desktop scanning of photographs. First, the shadow areas often scan much too flat, so you lose a lot of detail. Second, the image for some weird reason (we've been trying to figure it out for years now) is almost always blurry.

Almost every gray-scale scan we create around here immediately goes through a quick postscan process in Adobe Photoshop (although you can do essentially the same thing in other image manipulation programs).

1. We open the file in Adobe Photoshop and take quick readings of gray levels.

2. If the image needs it (it usually does), we boost the shadows with the Levels feature so that the black areas lighten to about 94 percent.

3. Then we sharpen the image. Different people have different ways of doing this, but we usually use the Unsharp Masking filter once or twice.

4. Finally, we save the file as a TIFF (depending on how much space we have on our hard disks that day, we might save it with LZR compression).

This process usually results in a good image (see Figure 7-2).

FIGURE 7-2
Scanned images
before and after
processing in
Adobe
Photoshop

HALFTONES

Let's face it. Every high-resolution imagesetter on the market prints only in black and white. And almost every low-resolution laser printer prints only in black and white. There's clearly a lot to be said for black and white. What we need to realize, however, is that black and white is not gray. Real laser printers don't print gray.

So how do we get a picture that contains grays into the computer and out onto paper? The answer is halftones. The magic of half-toning is that different levels of gray are represented by differently sized cells, which, when printed closely together, fool the eye into seeing the tint we want.

Take a look at any photograph in a newspaper, and it's easy to see the halftoning. Notice that the spacing of the cells doesn't change; only their size changes. There are large spots in dark areas, small spots in light areas (see Figure 7-3). Let's take a look at the elements that make up digital halftones.

Dots. A laser printer prints pages by placing black dots on a white page (remember, this is the simple approach, and we're not getting into film negatives yet). Each and every dot on a 300-dpi printer is going to be $\frac{1}{300}$ of an inch (or thereabouts) in diameter. That's pretty small, but it's still 8.5 times larger than what you can achieve on a Linotronic 300 ($\frac{1}{2,540}$ of an inch, which is almost too small for the human eye to see). The primary factor affecting the size of the dot is the resolution of the printer (how many dots per inch it can print).

Cells. As I said before, a halftone is made up of cells of varying sizes. On a black-and-white laser printer or imagesetter, these cells are created by bunching together anywhere between one and 65,000 printer dots. They can be of different shapes and (to be redundant over and over again) different sizes. For example, most halftone cells

FIGURE 7-3
Halftones are
made of cells

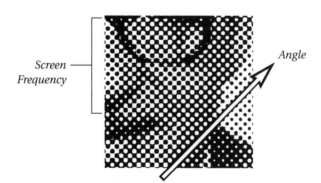

*Screen
Frequency*

Angle

are circular. However, programs like QuarkXPress let you change a halftone cell's shape to a line, a square, or an ellipse (see Figure 7-4). Another word for a halftone cell is a halftone spot.

FIGURE 7-4
Halftone
cell shape

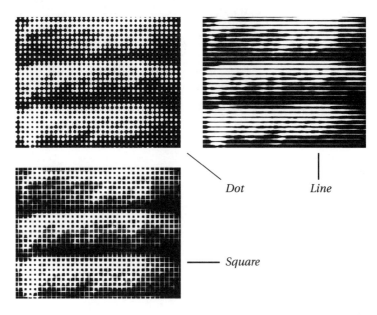

Dot   *Line*

Square

Screen frequency. In the traditional halftoning process, a mesh-like screen is placed in front of the photograph to create the desired effect of cells arranged in rows. Keeping that process in mind can help you understand this concept: the screen frequency of a halftone is set by the mesh-like screen, and is defined as the number of these rows or lines per inch (lpi). The lower the screen frequency, the coarser the image looks. The higher the screen frequency, the finer the image looks (see Figure 7-5). The screen frequency is often called its line screen. Whatever you call it, it's still specified in the number of lines per inch (lpi). See Table 7-1 for information about when to use a particular line screen.

Angle. The halftone screen does not have to be horizontal or vertical. It can rotate to other angles as well (see Figure 7-6), which can be of great use in both special-effects halftoning and color separation (see Chapter 9, *Printing*). For the sake of reference, 0 and

FIGURE 7-5
Various screen
frequencies

20 lpi   *75 lpi*   *120 lpi*

TABLE 7-1
When to use a
line screen

Output	Lines per inch
Photocopier	50–90 lpi
Newspaper quality	60–85 lpi
Quick-print printer	85–110 lpi
Direct mail pieces	110–150 lpi
Magazine quality	133–185 lpi
Art book	185–300 lpi

180 degrees are horizontal, 90 and 270 degrees are vertical (some types of cells look the same at all four of these angles, and others look very different at each angle). A 45-degree angle is used most commonly, primarily because it is the least distracting to the eye. Remember that changing the angle of the halftone screen doesn't change the angle of the picture itself!

**GRAY LEVELS
IN YOUR
HALFTONES**

Picture this: each cell is made up of tiny dots, and different gray levels are produced by turning various dots on and off (in a 10-percent tint, 10 percent of the dots within a cell are turned on). Okay, now remember that the lower the screen frequency, the bigger the cell, and the more dots used per cell. Likewise: the higher the frequency, the fewer dots used. Thus, when the screen frequency is higher, there are fewer possibilities for levels of gray (see Figure 7-7).

FIGURE 7-6
Halftone angles

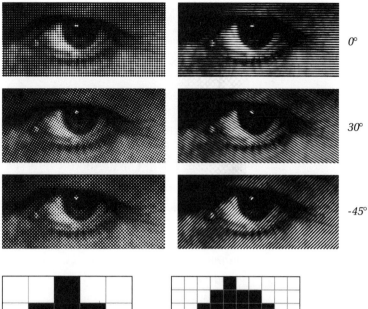

0°

30°

-45°

FIGURE 7-7
Halftone gray
levels

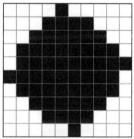

Halftone cell made of 25 dots at 50% gray (half the dots are "turned on"). Only 26 levels of gray are possible here.

Halftone cell made of 100 dots at 50% gray. This halftone cell can produce 101 levels of gray.

To find out how many levels of gray you can produce, divide the resolution by the screen frequency, square it, and add one. For example, you can get 92 levels of gray when you print a 133-line screen at 1,270 dpi (1,270 divided by 133 equals 9.55; this squared, plus one, equals 92); but you can get only 6 levels of gray when you print a 133-line screen at 300 dpi. The output is clearly posterized. To get 92 levels of gray on a 300-dpi laser printer, you would need to print at 30 lines per inch! It's an unfortunate fact, but this is one of the inherent tradeoffs in digital halftoning.

OTHER SCANNING ISSUES

Earlier in this chapter, I brought up an example of scanning a 2-by-2-inch piece of line art. Now, let's look more closely at scanning continuous-tone images (this discussion also applies to creating synthetic bitmapped images). Remember that when you scan smart with continuous-tone images (such as photographs), you need to ask yourself a series of questions before starting.

Pixel depth. First, how many levels of gray can the printer handle? If you're printing to a desktop laser printer that can only print a handful of gray levels, you probably don't need to scan the image at higher than 4 bits (16 gray levels). However, if your final art is printed from an imagesetter, you probably want to scan the image at 8 bits (256 gray levels).

Resolution. Second, what resolution should you scan at? When you're printing a halftone, you want the bitmapped image to have a resolution twice the screen frequency you're printing at. For example, if your halftone has a line screen of 65 lines per inch (lpi), your bitmapped image should have a resolution of 130 dpi. Any less, and your image quality may suffer. Any more, and you're just wasting space and printing time. This is called twice sampling.

Let's say you're creating an image with Adobe Photoshop that you're going to send to a film recorder (to make a 35mm slide). Film recorders (such as the Agfa Matrix SlideWriter or the Lasergraphics LFR) print continuous tones rather than halftones. That is, printing a 50-percent gray on a laser printer gives you a 50-percent halftone dot. But printing it on a film recorder gets you a flat 50-percent gray color. Therefore, your primary concern with film recorders is not screen frequency, but the grain of the film and of the imaging tube. To fully discuss the issues here would take more time than it's presently worth. Suffice it to say that to scan smart in the wild world of film recorders, you'll need to do some testing.

Dimensions. Third, what size do you need to scan at? Many scanning software packages let you specify the dimensions of the finished scan (regardless of the size of art you're scanning). For example, if you're scanning a 4-by-5-inch photograph, you can tell the scanning software to create a 2-by-3-inch scan (at a specific resolution). I generally like to scan artwork to the size it will be in its finished printed form. However, if I don't know how large the finished piece will be, I would prefer to scan it with larger rather than smaller dimensions. For example, if I know that the finished piece will be somewhere between 2 and 5 inches wide, I'll probably scan it to 5 inches wide. That way, I'll never need to enlarge the image, thus reducing my resolution.

BITMAPPED IMAGES WITH TEXT

At the beginning of this chapter, I talked about the guy who tried to read a gray-scale scan of a page of text with a word processor. As you can see in Figure 7-8, what he saw didn't help him much. The step he was skipping was to process his scan with optical character recognition (OCR) software.

FIGURE 7-8
Bitmapped
images of text
aren't really text

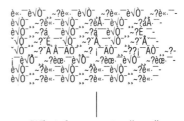

What the scan looks like   *What the computer "sees"*

OPTICAL
CHARACTER
RECOGNITION

As I said earlier: to a computer, all scans are just sets of dots—the computer has no way of telling what the image is. In order for the computer to translate a scanned page of text into real text that you can edit or format, you must process the scan through optical character recognition (OCR) software.

Most OCR programs work by "looking" at the scan, trying to figure out what parts of the picture are likely to be letters or numbers, and then building a text file based on what it finds. Each time the program finds something that looks like a letter or a number, it compares it to other letters that it knows. For example, if it sees something that is fairly circular but has a line going through the middle, it has to decide whether the character is an "o," an "e," or an "ø."

Because the software depends on these look-up tables to figure out what each character actually is, there are many typefaces or character formats that the computer won't be able to translate properly. For example, if the computer doesn't know what the letter "A" looks like in a script typeface, it won't give you an "A" (see Figure 7-9). Monospaced typefaces such as Courier or Letter Gothic generally scan relatively well with many OCR systems. Some OCR programs (such as ReadIt) let you teach them new typefaces and type styles.

FIGURE 7-9
Optical character recognition

Seattle, WA 98195

Spring

The computer scan (what the computer "sees")

Seattle, WA   98195

Spring

The equivalent characters in the OCR software's look-up table

Seactle, VA   98195

Spn@ry

The output from the OCR software (the "@" represents an unknown character)

CHAPTER 8

COLOR

𝕏𝕄𝕏𝕄𝕏𝕄𝕏𝕄𝕏𝕄𝕏𝕄𝕏𝕄𝕏𝕄𝕏𝕄𝕏𝕄𝕏𝕄𝕏𝕄𝕏𝕄

WHAT'S INSIDE

▶ The colors you see on your computer screen are almost never what you'll get on your output.

▶ An important distinction between kinds of printed color on the Mac is the difference between spot color and process color.

▶ Spot colors are usually defined as RGB, HSB, or Pantone colors.

▶ Process colors are usually defined either as CMYK (cyan, magenta, yellow, and black), or Trumatch colors.

▶ Trapping and overprinting are used to counter misregistration on a printing press.

If it weren't so sad, it would really be pretty funny. Just as soon as all these designers and ad agencies had gotten the hang of typography on the Macintosh, they all said (in unison), "Okay! Let's do all our color work on the Mac, too!"

Four cases of aspirin and six consultants later, all that was left was a tired pile of disillusioned production staff and a deadline approaching like an angry water buffalo.

Let's be realistic for a moment. If you haven't learned this already, listen closely now: working with color on a personal computer is not easy. In fact, it's downright tricky. If you follow the directions and leave the settings at their defaults, your job will probably look like mud. Even if you've worked as a color stripper for twenty years, if you don't understand this technology your job probably won't even print.

So, can you win? Is there even any point in trying? Absolutely. In this chapter we discuss the present-day limits of desktop color and how you can make it work for you. I'm not going to talk about "good color" versus "bad color," or what your job should look like. That's for you and your eyeballs (or your art director's eyeballs) to decide. Also, we won't talk too much about color separation yet; that's covered in Chapter 9, *Printing*. For now, we'll concentrate on how the computer handles color.

WHAT YOU SEE AND WHAT YOU GET

Before we even begin talking desktop color, it's important for you to know that the color you see on the screen is almost never what you'll get from your color printer or slide recorder, much less what you can expect to see on a printing press. Why? The primary reason is the difference in medium. Colors are displayed on the screen by lighting up phosphors, which emit colored light, which then enters your eyes. This is significantly different from colored printed material, which depends on other light sources to reflect off of it into your eyes. If you use a different method of showing color, you'll see different colors.

Pantone colors are a great example of this: take a Pantone swatchbook and pick a color. Hold that color next to a Pantone color simulation on the screen. Chances are it'll be a totally different color. Even color proofs created from your final film aren't completely reliable (though they're the best predictor you can hope for, outside of a press proof). What comes off the press may look different.

Another reason for the difference in color correspondence is that representing four process-color plates (cyan, magenta, yellow, and black) with three colors (red, green, and blue) just doesn't work. The eye sees and processes the two differently.

Want more reasons? Okay, how about the monitors and imaging devices themselves? Take a color document from your color Macintosh and bring it to someone else's computer; it almost undoubtedly looks different, especially if the monitor is a different brand. Take that a step farther, and image the document using a high-end slide recorder: the device uses light, just like your monitor, but the colors you get from it are often very different from what you see on your computer.

Some monitors are better than others at displaying certain colors. And a monitor with a 24-bit color card is probably one step more accurate than an 8-bit video card. Some companies, such as Barco, sell monitor-calibration systems to adjust the screen colors so that they'll more closely match your printed output. However, many of the best calibration systems are cost-prohibitive for most people.

Whatever you use, remember that what you see is rarely what you actually get.

The way out of all this uncertainty is to specify your colors from a swatchbook. Look at the book, see what color you want, and spec it. If possible, create your own swatchbook, and print it on your final output device—offset press, color printer, slide recorder, whatever. If you're printing process color, spec your colors from a process-color swatch book. If you're printing PMS color, use a PMS book.

DESCRIBING COLOR

In a perfect world you should be able to say, "I want this color to be burnt sienna," and your computer, service bureau, and lithographer would know exactly the color you mean. Outside of picking Crayola crayon colors, however, this just can't be done. Everyone, from scientists to artists to computer programmers, has been trying for centuries to come up with a general model for specifying and recreating colors. In the past 50 years alone, these color models have been created: HSB, NTSC, CMYK, YIQ, CIE, PAL, HSL, RGB, CCIR, RS-170, UVL, and HSI, among others. (And we thought that Macintosh graphic file format names were far out!)

To work with color on the Macintosh, you need to know about and understand four color models, plus two color-matching systems (we'll describe the difference later): RGB, CMY, CMYK, HSB, plus Pantone and Trumatch. Because these color models are intimately connected with printing and other reproduction methods, we'll first discuss the particulars of printing color, then move into each color model in turn.

SPOT VERSUS PROCESS COLOR

When dealing with color, either on the desktop or off, you need to understand the differences between process color and spot color. Both are commonly used in the printing business. Both can give you a wide variety of colors. But they are hardly interchangeable. Depending on your final output device, you may also be dealing with composite colors. Let's look at each of these, one at a time.

Process color. Look at any color magazine or junk mail you've received lately. If you look closely at a color photograph or a tinted color box, you'll probably see lots of little dots making up the color. These are color halftones made up of one, two, three, or four colors: cyan, magenta, yellow, and black. We'll talk about this color model (CMYK) a little later on; what's important here is that many, many colors are being simulated by overlapping four basic colors. The eye blends these colors together so that ultimately you see the color you're supposed to.

Cyan, magenta, yellow, and black are the process colors. The method of separating the millions of possible colors into only four is referred to as creating process color separations. Each separation—sometimes known as a plate—is a piece of film or paper that contains artwork for only one of the colors. Your lithographer can take the four pieces of film, burn a metal plate from each of the four pieces, and use those four plates on a four-color printing press.

Don't get us wrong: process color is not just for full-color photographs or images. If you're printing a four-color job, you can use each of the process colors separately or together to create colored type, rules, or tint blocks on the page. These items appear as solid colors to the untrained eye, but are actually "tint builds" of the process colors.

Spot color. If you are printing only a small number of colors (three or fewer), you probably want to use spot color. The idea behind spot color is that the printing ink (or light source, if you're printing to color slides) is exactly the color you want, which makes the need to build a color (using the four process colors) unnecessary. With spot color, if you want some text to be colored teal blue, you imageset it on a plate (often called an overlay) separate from the black plate. Your lithographer prints that text using teal blue ink—probably a PMS color (see "Pantone," below) like PMS 3135 or 211—and then switches to black to print the rest of the job.

Once again, the difference between process and spot color is that process colors are built using tints of four separate colors printed on top of each other, while spot colors are printed using just one colored ink (the color you specify). In either case, your lithographer runs the same page through the press more than once—one pass for each color—or uses a multicolor press that prints the colors successively on a single pass.

Mixing the two together. There is no reason why you can't use both spot and process color together in a document, if you've got the budget for a five- or six-color print job. Some lithographers have five- or six-color presses, which can print the four process colors along with one or two spot colors, or a varnish.

Composite color. If your final output is created on a film recorder (which produces slides or transparencies) or a color printer, you may well encounter what I call composite color. Composite color is color which falls between spot color and process color. For example, most film recorders print using the RGB format (see "RGB," below), whether your color is specified as CMYK or RGB or anything else your software allows you to do. Similarly, the QMS ColorScript 100 color printer represents both spot and process colors alike using either RGB or CMYK, depending on what type of wax-transfer colors you have loaded.

The key here is that the colors you specify are being represented using some color model which you may not have intended. If you know that you are printing on such a device, you should refer to the service bureau and/or to the owner's manual for tips on how to work best with that device.

COLOR MODELS

The next step we need to take in understanding color on the Macintosh is discussing color models. As I noted above, you really only need to understand four color models (RGB, CMY, CMYK, and HSB), plus two color-matching systems (Pantone and Trumatch). Let's look at each of these and what they're good for.

RGB. Color models are broken down into two classes: additive systems and subtractive systems. An additive color system is counter-intuitive to most people: the more color you add to an object, the closer you get to white. In the case of the RGB model, adding 100 percent each of red, green, and blue to an area results in pure white. If you have a color television, or a color monitor on your computer, you have already had a great deal of experience with the RGB model. These pieces of equipment describe colors by "turning on" red, green, and blue phosphors on the screen. Various colors are created by mixing these three colors together.

▶ Black=zero percent of all three colors

▶ Yellow=red + green

▶ Magenta=red + blue

▶ Cyan=green + blue

Color TIFF files, such as scans of natural images, are often saved using RGB specs. Most slide recorders image film using this method.

CMY. Subtractive colors, on the other hand, become more white as you subtract color from them, and get darker as you add more color. This is analogous to painting on a white piece of paper. CMY is a subtractive color model: the more cyan, magenta, and yellow you add together, the closer to black you get.

The connection between RGB and CMY is interesting: they are exact opposites of each other. In other words, you can take an RGB color, mathematically invert each of the RGB values, and get the same color in the CMY model. If this doesn't come intuitively to you (it doesn't to us), don't worry. The theory behind this is much less important than what it implies.

The implication of RGB and CMY having an inverse relationship is that colors in either model should be easy to convert. This is true. The problem is that the CMY model has few practical applications because cyan, magenta, and yellow don't really add up to make black in the real world. They make a muddy brown. Thus, lithographers over the years have learned that they must add a black element to the printing process.

CMYK. The color model that results when black is added to the CMY model is called CMYK. And whereas RGB is a standard for phosphorous screens, CMYK is the standard in the printing world, and is the basis of color separations. It breaks down any color into four basic colors: cyan, magenta, yellow, and black ("K" is used in the acronym rather than "B," to avoid confusion with "blue"). However, the conversion between RGB and CMYK is nowhere near as precise as one would hope. In fact, different programs use different conversion algorithms, so an RGB color in QuarkXPress prints differently from the way it would in FreeHand.

You can describe many colors using the CMYK method. This is how Quark describes a few, to the nearest percentage.

▶ Red=100 percent magenta + 30 percent yellow

▶ Green=77 percent cyan + 100 percent yellow

▶ Blue=100 percent cyan + 96 percent magenta

Almost every full-color job that gets printed on paper uses the CMYK process.

HSB. Rather than breaking a color down into subparts, the HSB model describes a color by its hue, saturation, and brightness. The hue is basically its position on a color spectrum which starts at red, moves through violet to blue, through green to yellow, and then through orange back to red. The saturation of the color can be described as the amount of color in it. Or, conversely, the amount of white in it. Light pink, for example, has a lower saturation than bright red. The color's brightness has to do with the amount of black in it. Thus, that same bright red would, with a lower brightness level, change from a vibrant red to a dark, dull, reddish-black.

You could also say that mixing a color (hue) with white produces a tint (a degree of saturation). Mixing it with black produces a tone (a degree of brightness).

HSB is not easy to understand intuitively, especially when it comes to specifying colors. For example, here are the hue values for the same colors specified above.

▶ Red=0

▶ Green=21,845 (or 33.3 percent)

▶ Blue=43,690 (or 66.7 percent)

You may find speccing HSB useful if you're creating slides on a film recorder or the like, but it's not much use in print publishing.

Pantone. One of the many subsidiaries of Esselte, the largest graphic design supplier in the world, is Pantone, Inc., whose sole purpose in life (and business) is to continue to develop, maintain, and protect the sanctity of the Pantone Color Matching System (PMS for short).

Printers and designers alike love the PMS system for its great simplicity in communicating color. As a designer, you can look in a Pantone-approved color swatchbook, pick a color, then communicate that color's number to your printer. He or she, in turn, can pull out the Pantone color mixing guidelines, find that color's "recipe," and dutifully create it for you. Almost all spot-color printing in the U. S. is done with PMS inks.

Bear in mind that you can simulate many PMS colors using combinations of process inks. Some simulations are better than others. A pale blue is fairly easy to simulate with process inks, for instance; a rich, creamy, slate blue is almost impossible; and you'll never get anything approaching copper or gold with CMYK.

Pantone, knowing a good thing when it sees it, has licensed its color library to many software developers so that you can specify PMS colors from within their products. However, the color you see on the screen when you select a Pantone color may have little correlation to what the actual PMS color looks like on paper. A computer screen is no substitute for a swatchbook (I'll talk more about this later).

There are three problems with PMS color.

▶ Only certain colors are defined and numbered. If you want a color which is slightly lighter than one described, but not as light as the next lightest color in the Pantone book, you have to tell your lithographer to tweak it.

▶ Color specification books are never fully accurate or alike. I work with a Pantone book which is almost totally different from my printer's, due mostly to the difference in the age of the books, the ink types, and the paper types the books are printed on.

▶ I've never met anyone who actually understood the PMS numbering scheme. For example, PMS 485 and PMS 1795 are very similar, though every number in between is totally different.

On the other hand, some designers use Pantone colors to avoid some pitfalls that process colors create. For example, the Understanding Company creates roadmaps that are often designed and printed using one to five Pantone inks in various tints and combinations. This minimizes both the potential moiré patterning (see Chapter 9, *Printing*), and the possible loss of detail in small colored type.

Remember that the Pantone system is really designed for color matching, rather than describing a color abstractly like these other color models do.

Trumatch. The newest entry into the color-matching systems, and the only one that was developed using desktop technology, is Trumatch. This matching system is similar to Pantone in that you and your printer each have Trumatch books that you can pick particular colors out of. However, Trumatch is based not on solid spot colors that can be cooked up by your printer, but on builds of process colors.

The colors in the Trumatch swatchbook are arranged in the colors of the spectrum: from red through yellow to green through blue to violet and back to red. The first number in the Trumatch code is a color's hue (its place on the spectrum). These numbers go from 1 to 50.

The second item in a color's Trumatch code is its tint (its value strength). These are labeled from "a" (saturated, 100-percent value strength) to "h" (faded, unsaturated, 5-percent value strength). The third item is the color's brightness (the amount of black in it). Black is always added in 6-percent increments. The shade code ranges from 1 (6 percent black) to 7 (42 percent black). If there's no black in a color, this third code is left off.

So, why is this so great? Well, first of all, you can quickly make decisions on the relativity of two colors. For example, you can say "No, I want this color to be a little darker, and a little more green," and then quickly come up with a new color. Compare this to the Pantone Matching System and you'll understand. Trumatch gives us hope that there really is a positive evolution in electronic publishing.

COLOR TRICKS THE EYE

Placing a colored object next to a different colored object makes both colors look different from how each would if you just had one color alone. Similarly, a color can look totally different if you place it on a black background rather than on a white one. These facts should influence how you work in two ways. First, when you're selecting colors from a swatchbook, isolate the colors from their neighbors. I like to do this by placing a piece of paper with a hole cut out of it in front of a color we're considering. Secondly, after you've created the colors you're going to work with in your document, try them out with each other. You may find that you'll want to go back and edit them in order to create the effect you really want.

TRAPPING

Nothing is perfect, not even obscenely expensive printing presses. When your print job is flying through those presses, each color being added one at a time, the paper may shift slightly. Depending on the press, this could be a shift of anywhere between .003 and .0625 inch (.2 to 4.5 points). If two colors abut each other on your artwork and this shift occurs, then the two colors may be moved apart slightly, resulting in an unprinted white space. It may seem like a 3/1000-inch space would look like a small crack in a large sidewalk, but we assure you, it could easily appear to be a chasm. What can you do? Fill in these potential chasms with traps and overprints.

The concept and execution of traps and overprints contain several potential pitfalls for the inexperienced. Up until now, most designers just let their lithographers and strippers handle it. There is a school of thought that says we should still let them handle it. But you know these desktop publishers; they always want to be in control of everything. The problem is that designers weren't trained to do trapping! Let's look carefully at what overprinting and trapping are all about.

Overprinting. Picture the letter "Q," colored magenta on a cyan background. Normally, when creating color separations, the cyan plate (we'll talk more about color separations and plates in Chapter 9, *Printing*) has a white "Q" knocked (reversed) out of it, exactly where the magenta "Q" prints. This way the cyan and the magenta don't mix (see Figure 8-1). You can, however, set the magenta to overprint the cyan. This results in the "Q" not being knocked out of the cyan; the two colors overprint in that area, resulting in a purple "Q" on a cyan background.

FIGURE 8-1
Knockouts and
overprinting

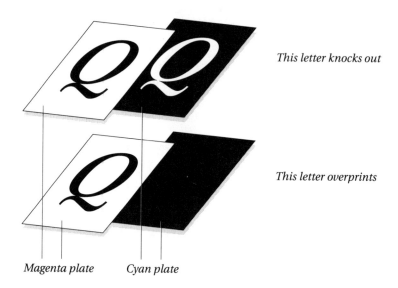

This letter knocks out

This letter overprints

Magenta plate   *Cyan plate*

Trapping. A trap is created by overprinting two colors very slightly, along their borders. Then, if (or when) the paper shifts in the printing press, the space between the colors is filled in with the additional trap color rather than white (see Figure 8-2). The trap can be created using two methods: choking and spreading. Choking refers to the background area getting smaller. Spreading refers to the foreground object (in the above example, the "Q") getting slightly larger.

Simple idea, right? But not necessarily a simple process when you're just beginning.

FIGURE 8-2
Trapping fills in
the cracks

Untrapped

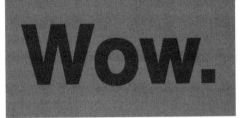

Trapped

**TRAPPING
AND OVER-
PRINTING
SMALL TYPE**

You can run into trouble when you're using small type, especially serif type, in a color document. Since the type is so fine—especially the serifs—even a small amount of trapping can clog it up. The counters (the open areas, like the inside of a lowercase "a") can fill in, and the serifs can get clunky (see Figure 8-3). Bear this in mind when you're setting up your trapping preferences, and when you're specifying colors for type.

FIGURE 8-3
Trapping type

Monsieur de Bergerac   *Untrapped*

Monsieur de Bergerac   *Trapped*

Overprinting can also be treacherous. For example, if you overprint red on blue, you get purple, which is probably not what you intended.

There are a few very important times when you'll want to overprint colors. The most important of these times, perhaps, is printing fine black lines or type on a colored background. In fact, almost any time you have a black foreground object, it should overprint the background.

FOUR-COLOR BLACK

Even better, you can create a much richer black color by defining a separate black in your color palette which contains a bit of other process color in it. The standard rich black that color strippers use is 100 percent black along with 40 percent cyan. Some people like to get complicated, though, and add 20 to 30 percent each of magenta and yellow, too. When a plain black (100 percent K) object overlaps colored objects like photographs, its density shifts, depending on whether it's over a light or dark area. Adding color to your blacks solves the problem.

This trick works not only for achieving richer black on a printing press, but also better blacks from a thermal color printer like the ColorScript 100. However, if the thermal color printer is your final destination, you might boost the additional colors to between 50 and 100 percent each.

Note, though, that you should think carefully about how you apply this rich black. A potential problem lurks behind this technique: the cyan can show up from behind the black if (or when) the printing press misregisters.

CHAPTER 9

PRINTING

WHAT'S INSIDE

▶ If a printer font is not available for a typeface in your document, when you print it will come out looking wrong.

▶ You use the Chooser to tell your software where to print your file.

▶ You use the Page Setup dialog box to tell your software about both the printer and how you want your job to print.

▶ The Print dialog box gives you more options for printing your document, including the number of copies and the page range.

▶ Other considerations when printing are registration marks, tiling, color separations, and dot gain.

▶ When working with a service bureau, you need to know how to send your files. You may want to send PostScript print-to-disk files.

▶ Other considerations when working with a service bureau are compatibility, large file sizes, and their equipment.

So you've got this white piece of paper. And you've got this disk with a beautiful-looking document on it. And everyone says, "Just choose Print from the File menu and click OK." No pain. No hassle. The computer has made this last step as easy as can be, right? Wrong.

The amount of time you've put into creating your document is directly proportional to the amount of time you should think carefully about how it's being printed. That is, if you've used Microsoft Word to throw together a quick one-page handout, you can go ahead and just print the thing on your laser printer without a second thought. On the other hand, if you've worked for three months producing a four-hundred-page book, you had better be careful and methodical in your printing process.

In this chapter I'll discuss every aspect of printing a job, from the Chooser through Page Setup to pressing OK in the Print dialog box. Then I'll discuss other aspects of print jobs, such as registration marks, color separations, and working with service bureaus.

Before I get into anything too complex, though, let's deal with two simple yet crucial issues in most people's print jobs: PostScript and fonts.

POSTSCRIPT

To put it simply, PostScript is what makes desktop publishing on the Macintosh possible. PostScript is a page-description language—a set of commands that PostScript laser printers understand. When you tell your Macintosh to print a page, it writes a program in PostScript describing the page, and sends that program to the printer. The printer (or imagesetter), which has a PostScript interpreter inside it, interprets the PostScript program describing the page, and puts text and images on the paper (or film) according to that description.

Not everyone who uses the Macintosh needs to use PostScript, but it's become a standard in the desktop publishing community. Therefore, I'm going to assume you're working with an Adobe

PostScript printer. If you're working with a clone interpreter, such as the RIPS, Freedom of the Press, or GoScript, I take no responsibility for what comes out on paper. The only reason I use clone interpreters is to laugh at the mistakes they make. Things change fast in this business, of course; there may be some good clones out there by the time you read this.

As Adobe's advertisements tell us, PostScript is the creamy filling in the Oreo cookie. However, this creamy PostScript filling that makes the printer so desirable also makes a printer significantly more expensive. If you can't afford a PostScript printer, you should do three things.

▶ Start saving your shekels so you can buy one soon.

▶ Don't expect to do high-quality graphic work (it's possible, but not very easy).

▶ Read this chapter (I talk a lot about PostScript, but that's not all I talk about!).

FONTS

Almost everyone uses the Macintosh at some point to work with text. It's a given. When you work with text, you work with typefaces (fonts).

If you don't fully understand how bitmapped and outline fonts work together, I recommend that you go back and look over the beginning of Chapter 3, *Fonts*. Working with fonts requires a slightly different approach to the printing process.

PRINTING FONTS

Bitmapped fonts work in tandem with outline fonts. The Macintosh automatically replaces the bitmapped screen font with the outline font at print time. But to be able to make this switch, it must be able to find the outline printer font—either in the printer's permanent memory, or in a file on disk.

The Macintosh first queries the printer to see if it has the font loaded in memory, in ROM (the printer's permanent memory), or on a hard disk attached to the printer. If the font can't be found in any of these places, the Macintosh looks in the current system folder for the font. If you're using Suitcase II or MasterJuggler, the Macintosh also looks in the same folder as the screen font you have loaded.

Next, assuming that the Macintosh can find the printer font, it downloads the font information to the laser printer along with your document. PostScript laser printers have memory allocated for font storage. However, printer models vary in their memory allocations, and thus in the number of fonts they can hold. For example, the old LaserWriters could only keep three or four fonts in memory at a time, while an Apple LaserWriter IINTX can keep about 12 or 13 fonts in memory. Exceeding the amount of memory available causes a PostScript error, flushing your job and restarting the printer (see Chapter 10, *When Things Go Worng*).

Note that you don't need the outline printer fonts in your system folder for any font that is resident in your printer. For example, all PostScript printers come with Times, Helvetica, Courier, and Symbol encoded directly into the printer's memory, so you don't need a printer font to use these typefaces (though you do need the printer font for ATM or TrueType to work correctly). The page that prints out when you start up your printer usually can tell you which fonts are resident.

PRINTING UGLY

When you have neither a printer font nor a printer-resident font available, the Macintosh has two options.

▶ Print using the Courier typeface. This usually happens when your document contains an EPS file with fonts that you don't have available.

▶ Print the text using the bitmapped screen font. The Macintosh prints the text almost exactly as it appears on screen.

I'm not sure which of these is uglier. I tend to break into hives at the sight of either one.

FONT DOWNLOADING

Ordinarily, when your printing job is done, the fonts that you used are flushed out of the printer's memory. Then, next time you print the document, the Macintosh has to download the fonts all over again. Downloading once may not seem like a long process, but having to download the fonts repeatedly starts to make chess look like a fast sport.

But you don't have to wait. You can do something about your predicament. You can download the fonts yourself.

Manual downloading. You can download a typeface to your printer and make it stay there until you turn the printer off. There are several utilities that let you do this. I like LaserStatus because it's a DA and because it's from CE Software (the makers of some of the world's coolest utilities). However, you can also use Adobe's Font Downloader or Apple's LaserWriter Font Utility.

Downloading a font manually is particularly helpful for typefaces which you use many times throughout the day. If Goudy is your corporate typeface, you can manually download it from one computer at the start of each day. And, as long as no one resets the printer, you can use it to your heart's content from any of the computers hooked up to the network (whether or not they have Goudy's printer font on their hard disks; but they do need to have the printer font installed).

Hard disk storage. If you have a hard disk connected to your printer, you have one more option: downloading a printer font to the printer's hard disk. Once you download a font this way, it stays there until you erase it (or drop the hard drive on the ground). Downloading utilities such as Adobe's Font Downloader and Apple's Laser-Writer Font Utility have the extra features necessary for this task. If you have some odd sort of printer, you may have to get special software from the manufacturer.

CHOOSING A PRINTER

When deciding what kind of printer to print your document on, the most important feature to look at is imaging resolution. Whereas many high-resolution imagesetters offer a variety of resolutions, most desktop laser printers are happy only when they're printing 300 dots per inch. Table 9-1 lists several printers and their resolutions.

I (like most people) use a desktop laser printer to print proof copies of my documents before I send them to a service bureau to be imageset onto RC paper or film. Every once in a while I meet someone who prints first to an ImageWriter II or other QuickDraw printer, and then uses a service bureau to get PostScript laser proofs made. If you haven't got a laser printer yourself and are forced to do this, then so be it, but be sure to take some precautions (see "Switching Printer Types," below).

If you're working on a new system or are working with multiple types of printers, the first thing you need to do is be aware of how your Chooser is set. The Chooser is a desk accessory (DA)—part of the Macintosh system software that lets you choose what kind of printer you want to use. You can also specify which printer, if there is more than one on a network. You access it by selecting "Chooser" from the Apple menu (see Figure 9-1). The icons on the left are the types of printer drivers you have installed in your system folder (printer drivers tell your computer how to drive your printer). When you click on one, the computer asks you for more pertinent information in the rectangle on the right.

TABLE 9-1	Device	Printing resolutions in dpi
Higher quality jobs require higher resolution printing	Apple ImageWriter II	72, 144
	Desktop laser printers	300, 400, 600
	Linotronic 300/500	635, 1270, 2540
	Compugraphic CG9400	1200, 2400
	Linotronic 330/530	1270, 2540, 3386
	Agfa Matrix SlideWriter	2000, 4000

For example, if you click on the ImageWriter icon, you're asked which port the ImageWriter is attached to. If you click on the LaserWriter icon, you're asked which LaserWriter you want to use (even if only one printer is attached, you still need to select it by clicking on its icon before closing the DA). If you have a large AppleTalk network which is split up into zones, you may have to select a zone before selecting a printer. The changes take effect as soon as you close the Chooser window.

FIGURE 9-1
The Chooser

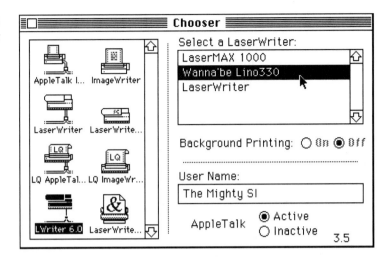

If you are working just with PostScript laser printers, you hardly need to worry about the Chooser. Just set it once and forget it, except when you want to switch between PostScript printers on the network.

SWITCHING PRINTER TYPES

If you are creating a document on a machine with one type of printer attached to it, then printing to a different printer for final output, make sure that you create your document with a printer driver compatible with the final output device. For example, if you are proofing on an ImageWriter II and will later print to a Linotronic imagesetter, create your entire document with a LaserWriter driver selected in the Chooser (you don't actually have to own the laser printer or have it on hand to use its driver). Then, when you want to print your document, switch to the ImageWriter driver, and don't change your Page Setup dialog box settings (see below). Call it superstition, or whatever you like, but it has taken care of some major printing problems for me in the past.

PAGE SETUP

Okay: you've got your document finished and you're ready to print. But wait! Don't forget to check the Page Setup dialog box.

The Page Setup dialog box varies slightly from one program to another, but it almost always contains four areas: paper specifications, printer effects, output effects, and options. Let's take a look at each of these in turn.

PAPER SPECIFICATIONS

Contrary to popular belief, the paper size that you choose in this area is not necessarily the page size of your document. It is, instead, the paper size onto which you want to print your document. For example, if your newsletter is set up on a regular 8.5-by-11-inch page, you can have it printed onto an area as large as a tabloid-size, or as small as a Number 10 envelope.

The paper size you choose determines the printing area. So, if you choose a Number 10 envelope from the pull-down menu (the one that's usually set up for Tabloid), but your document is actually larger than an envelope, your page is cropped down to 3.8 by 9.1 inches. (This also leaves a ⅛-inch border around the edge of the envelope; so no bleeds!).

PRINTER EFFECTS

This field encompasses four basic features, described below. All four default to On, but none of them has any consequence unless you're printing to a PostScript printer.

Font Substitution. Remember that New York, Geneva, and Monaco are not outline fonts, and they print out as bitmapped images on a PostScript printer (read: "ugly"). Checking "Font Substitution" allows the Macintosh to substitute Times Roman for New York, Helvetica for Geneva, and Courier for Monaco. Note that because the character widths for each font are different, your text almost always prints with the wrong character widths (see Figure 9-2).

Text Smoothing. If you must use a bitmapped font on a PostScript laser printer, you may want to enable Text Smoothing. This feature tells the printer to smooth out the bitmaps, so they don't look too jagged. I've seen both excellent and awful results with this. It works best with small-size fonts with few stair-stepped edges, and it's terrible with fonts that are out of their size ranges (that is, if you have a bitmapped font which was designed for 14 point and you're

FIGURE 9-2
Font
substitution

> I, sir, if that nose were mine,
> I'd have it amputated on the spot!

Typed in New York

I, sir, if that nose were mine,
I'd have it amputated on the spot!

Typed in New York, printed
with font substitution on

I, sir, if that nose were mine,
I'd have it amputated on the spot!

Typed in Times-Roman

using it at 39 point). In general, if it looks okay on the screen, it'll look at least decent in the output.

On the other hand, if you want the jaggy look of a bitmapped font, then be sure to disable the Text Smoothing feature. Many designers use the bitmapped quality as a design element (and the Text Smoothing feature makes their artwork look awful).

Graphics Smoothing. As the name would suggest, the Graphics Smoothing feature does to bitmapped graphics what Font Smoothing does to bitmapped fonts. This only works for Paint-type (PNTG) graphics (see Chapter 2, *Graphic File Formats*). Many people who are creating newsletters or flyers use this feature to smooth out inexpensive Paint-type clip art. There's no doubt that this helps a bit (okay, sometimes more than just a bit), but don't expect to get really smooth curves or diagonals from this feature. Also, if there are gray areas or patterns in the art, smoothing can really mess them up.

Faster Bitmap Printing. I can't be sure, but I think Faster Bitmap Printing is a feature that someone at Apple thought would be funny, so Apple included it in their Page Setup dialog box. Hey, who wouldn't want their bitmapped images to print faster? Why would anyone ever want to turn this off? In fact, turning it on does seem to speed up printing time from anywhere between .003 and 1 second on every test I've conducted. There is slightly more speedup if your bitmapped images have an integral relationship with the printer's resolution (for example, 75-dpi bitmapped images sometimes print better and faster than 72-dpi images, because 75 divides evenly into 300; though sometimes they don't). Whatever the case, the whole thing makes me nervous—always has—and I automatically turn this feature off when I print.

OUTPUT EFFECTS

You have control over two document-printing effects in this section of the Page Setup dialog box: reduction or enlargement, and orientation.

Reduce or Enlarge. Changing this number affects the scaling of the document when you print. You can enter any whole number (no decimal points) between 10 and 400 percent. This is especially nice when printing proofs of a larger-format document, or when trying to create enormous posters by tiling them. Table 9-2 shows several page-size conversion settings.

TABLE 9-2
Page sizes

To print this size page	On this size of paper	Reduce/enlarge to
legal	letter	78%
tabloid	letter	64%
A4	letter	94%
letter	tabloid	128%

Orientation. Remember the first day of high school, when they had Orientation Day? The idea was to make sure you knew which way you were going while walking around the school grounds. Well, this Orientation is sort of the same, but different. The idea is to make sure the Macintosh knows which way you want your document to go when it's walking through the printer. You have two choices: portrait and landscape. Luckily, this feature has its own icons so that you don't have to think too hard about which to choose. I've included some samples in Figure 9-3 so you can see what each one does.

When you're printing onto a roll-fed imagesetter, you can usually save film or paper by printing your letter-size pages landscape rather

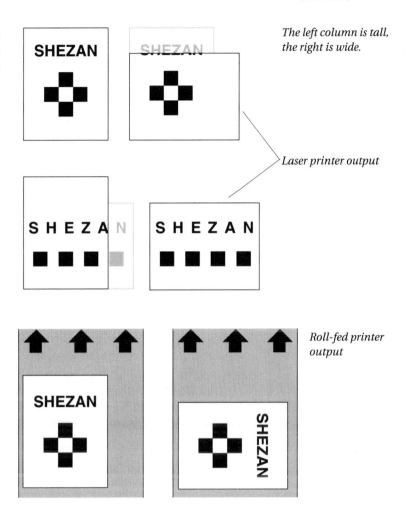

FIGURE 9-3
Tall versus wide
orientation

*The left column is tall,
the right is wide.*

Laser printer output

*Roll-fed printer
output*

than portrait. That way you only use about 8.5 inches on the roll rather than 11 inches. It may not seem like a great difference, but those two and a half inches really add up when you're printing a long document. For example, a hundred-page file will save an average of 250 inches of film or paper when printed in landscape orientation. Printing the pages landscape also makes it easy to cut them apart and stack them. Check with your service bureau to see if they'll give you a discount for the time and energy you've saved them.

OPTIONS

You can access a second page of Page Setup options by clicking on the Options button in the Page Setup dialog box (see Figure 9-4). The hallowed halls of Macintosh folklore may someday be cluttered with speculation on what particular animal is shown on this dialog box's page icon. While the consensus seems to be that it's a dog, I prefer to think it's the rare moof (half dog, half cow). Whatever the case, this is the animal to watch when it comes to five out of six of the features in Options.

FIGURE 9-4
Page Setup
Options

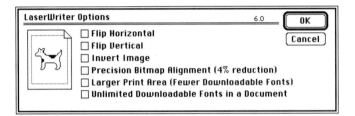

Flip Horizontal and Flip Vertical. I'll meld these two into one description, as they really do the same thing. Flipping an image is used primarily for creating from imagesetters either wrong- or right-reading film, or film with emulsion side up or down. The differences? Let's look at what happens when you print on film.

As the film moves through the imagesetter, the side of the film coated with a light-sensitive emulsion is exposed to a beam of laser light. If you have neither Flip Horizontal nor Flip Vertical selected, the film is imaged wrong-reading, emulsion down (which is right-reading when the emulsion is up). This means that when you are holding the film so that the type and graphics look right ("right-reading"), the emulsion of the film is facing you. If you select either Flip Horizontal or Flip Vertical, the film emerges right-reading, emulsion down. To look at it in a different way, this means that when you hold the film with the emulsion away from you, the text and graphics look correct ("right-reading"). See Figure 9-5 for a quick graphic reference.

If you want to know why you'd ever care whether the emulsion is up or down, check with your lithographer (and then talk to a screen printer; you'll see they need different film output, for similar but different reasons).

FIGURE 9-5
Flip Horizontal
and Flip Vertical

Standard setting.
Right-reading,
emulsion up.

Flip Horizontal.
Right-reading,
emulsion down.

Flip Vertical.
Right reading,
emulsion down.

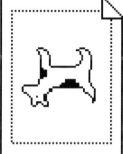

Flip Horizontal &
Flip Vertical.
Right reading,
emulsion up.

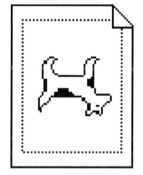

The bottom two
are essentially
the same as the
top two.

Invert Image. Clicking on this feature inverts the entire page so that everything set to 100 percent black becomes 0 percent black (effectively, white).

Precision Bitmap Alignment (4% reduction). The problem of printing bitmapped images, in a nutshell, is this: bitmapped images that don't have an integral relationship with the printer's resolution often print out with ugly tiled patterns. This is especially a problem with dithered black-and-white scans. For example, a 300-dpi printer attempting to print a 72-dpi picture has to resolve a discrepancy of

.17 point per inch (300 ÷ 72 = 4.17). When you select "Precision Bitmap Alignment," the entire document is scaled down 4 percent, which raises the effective resolution of the 72-dpi bitmap to almost 75 dpi, and that image now prints with few or no ugly patterns.

The problem is that now the rest of your document has been scaled down 4 percent. If you're printing a small company newsletter and you don't care how bad it looks (and all your bitmapped graphics happen to be 72 dpi), this might make no difference to you. Otherwise, it would be unwise to use this feature.

Larger Print Area (Fewer Downloadable Fonts). When you print a page to a desktop laser printer, you are only able to print up to approximately half an inch from the page edge because of the limited memory within the PostScript printer. The largest chunk of memory is reserved for storing the actual bitmapped image of the page. If you're working with a 300-dpi printer, it has to store around 7.5 million bits of information for each page it prints. The rest of the printer's memory is split up between the amount of space required to process the job (interpret the PostScript data) and to store the needed fonts.

By checking the Larger Print Area box, you tell the Mac to alter the memory allocation slightly, giving a bit more memory to the imageable area and a bit less to the font area. You can then print out to the very minimum quarter-inch border, but you have less room to store your downloadable fonts, so the number of downloadable fonts you can use on a page is reduced. In other words, a page which may print fine without the Larger Print Area box checked may now cause an overload in printer memory and a PostScript error.

Unlimited Downloadable Fonts in a Document. Checking this feature is a last resort when you really have too many fonts on a page to print it successfully. The issue here is time. Normally, the Macintosh downloads all the fonts it needs for a job as it needs them. If the printer's memory runs out, then it runs out, and you get a PostScript error telling you that you can't print the job.

If you have the Unlimited Downloadable Fonts in a Document feature enabled, the software you're using downloads the font when it needs it, then flushes it out of printer memory. Next time the document needs the font, the program downloads it again. The problem is, that might be 10 times on a single page, making your job print very slowly. So, while you gain the ability to print as many fonts as you want, you pay a hefty price in printing time.

PRINTING

Once you've got the proper values specified in the Page Setup dialog box, you can move on to the actual Print dialog box, again found under the File menu. Here you are confronted with even more buttons, controls, and special features designed to tweak your print job to the point of perfection. Each program may have its own Print dialog box, but there are some controls which are almost always present. Let's look at them one at a time.

Copies. I might as well start with the simplest choice of all. How many copies of your document do you want printed? Let's say you choose to print a multiple-page document and specify four copies. The first page prints four times, then the second page prints four times, and so on. In other words, you may have a good deal of collating to do later.

Pages. You can choose to print all pages of a document, or a range of pages. If you want to print from the first page to a specified page, you can leave the "From" field empty in the Print dialog box. Similarly, if you leave the "To" field empty, the Mac assumes you want to print to the end of the document.

Cover Page. This feature is usually set to "No," and I almost never change it. But then again, I don't work in large workgroups. Each cover sheet includes the name of the person who sent the job—determined by the name set in the Chooser DA—and a date and time stamp, along with other information. If you have several (or many) people printing to one printer, using cover sheets can be a real lifesaver. Not only does the cover page act as a label for each print job, but it separates each job so that a page from one document doesn't get mixed up with pages from the next document.

Note that you can set the cover page to print either before the first page or after the last page. Take your pick, depending on whether your printer dumps paper face up or face down. But if you're in a workgroup situation, you probably want everybody to use the same setting, to avoid confusion.

On the other hand, why use extra paper if you don't need to? If you're the only person using the printer, and you don't need to document each print cycle, just leave this feature turned off.

Paper Source. This feature specifies where you would like the printer to get its paper from. Normally you'd have this set to Paper Cassette. However, if you are using a printer that can take manually-fed pages, you may want to select this at various times—for example, when you print onto a single sheet of special stationery or onto an envelope.

When Manual Feed is selected, the printer waits for a designated time—usually 30 seconds or a minute—for you to properly place the sheet of paper in the manual feed slot. If you don't place the page in time, the PostScript interpreter reports a time-out error and flushes the rest of the print job.

Print. The last of Apple's standard Print dialog box settings identifies the type of printer you are using. Note that you will not see this item if you are using a LaserWriter driver earlier than version 6.0. You have two choices here.

▶ ***Color/Grayscale.*** Use this setting when printing to a printer capable of producing color or gray-scale tones; for example, the QMS ColorScript or the Océ Color Printer.

▶ ***Black & White.*** Here's the setting for the rest of us, when printing to a black-and-white printer (like just about anything you'd ordinarily print to). The difference is often negligible, but I recommend doing it to appease your computer.

OTHER PRINT CONSIDERATIONS

Before you go and start printing, there are a few other items that you should consider. In this section we'll take a look at registration marks, tiling, color separations, and dot gain. You may not need to use any of these…but then again, they might save your life one day.

REGISTRATION MARKS

In addition to the text and graphics on the pages themselves, your printer (I'm talking about the human lithographer here) needs several pieces of information about your camera-ready work. One is where the sides of the printed page are. If you're printing multiple colors, another piece of information your printer needs is how each color plate aligns with the other (I'll talk about creating color separations later in this chapter). Additional job and page information may be helpful also. Software such as PageMaker and Quark-XPress have features that create automatic trim marks (that show the edge of the page), registration marks (for color alignment), and job information (see Figure 9-6). If your software of choice can't create these, you may have to use whatever tools available in the program to create your own.

FIGURE 9-6
Registration and
crop marks

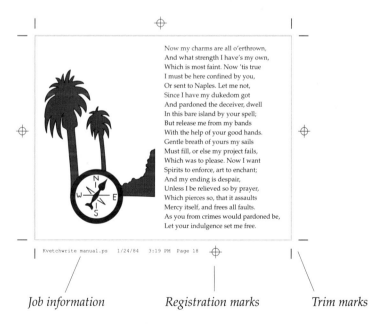

Job information   Registration marks   Trim marks

Crop marks specify the page boundaries of your document. They are placed slightly outside each of the four corners so that when the page is printed and cut to size, they will be cut away.

Registration marks are used primarily for color-separation work, but you get them even when you just need crop marks on a one-color job. These are used by your printer's stripper to perfectly align each color plate to the next.

TILING

What's a person to do with a 36-by-36-inch document? Printing to paper or film is...well, almost impossible. (To be thorough we should mention it can be done through the Scitex VIP interface to an ELP printer or on Colossal System's giant 300-dpi electrostatic printer.) You can break each page down into smaller chunks that will fit onto letter-size pages. Then you can assemble all the pages together (keep your Scotch tape nearby). This process is called tiling, and is usually controlled in the Print dialog box.

Most programs that can create pages larger than legal-size paper allow you to turn tiling on or off. And when it's turned on, you often have the choice between manual and automatic tiling. When you print with automatic tiling, the application figures out how to break the page down for you; the computer may print six pages to cover the area of your one large page. Manual tiling usually prints just one part of your page; you have to adjust the ruler origins in your document to tell the computer what part of the page you'd like to print. See your manual for a description of how to do this in your program.

COLOR SEPARATIONS

A printing press can only print one color at a time. Even five- and six-color presses really only print one color at a time, attempting to give the paper (or whatever) a chance to dry between coats. As I discussed back in Chapter 8, *Color*, those colors are almost always process colors (cyan, magenta, yellow, and black), or they may be spot colors, such as Pantone inks. Colors that you specify in your documents may look solid on the screen, but they need to be separated and imageset onto individual plates for printing. If your job contains only process colors, you output four pieces of film for every page of the document. Adding a spot color adds another plate to the lineup.

Another look at colors. If you haven't read Chapter 8, *Color*, I recommend you go back and look at it before getting deep into color separation. But given that you probably have as busy a schedule as I do, here's a quick rundown of the most important concepts.

▶ Process colors are colors that may look solid on the screen, but will break down into varying tints of cyan, magenta, yellow, and black, when printed as separations.

▶ Spot colors are colors which don't separate at print time. Instead, each prints on its own plate. These are typically Pantone (PMS) colors which will be printed with PMS inks.

▶ Each of the four process colors is printed as a halftone (if you don't understand the fundamentals of halftoning, I recommend you look at Chapter 7, *Scans & Halftones*). By overlapping the screened tints, a multitude of colors can be created.

The rosette. When the process color plates are laid down on top of each other, the halftones of each color mesh with each other in a subtle way. Each plate's halftone screen has a slightly different angle, and possibly a different frequency as well. The result is thousands of tiny rosette patterns (see Figure 9-7). If this process is done correctly, the separate colors blend together to form one apparently smooth, clean color. If the angles or screen frequency are slightly off, or the

FIGURE 9-7
The rosette

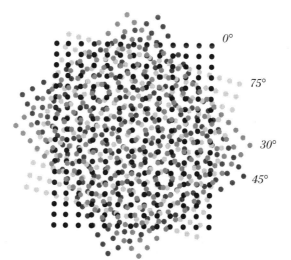

0°

75°

30°

45°

registration (alignment) of the plates is wrong, then all sorts of chaos can ensue. Both of these problems can come about from errors on the lithographer's part, but more likely they are problems with your imagesetting process.

The most common error is a pattern in the color called a moiré. There's almost no good way to describe a moiré pattern: it's best to just see a few of them. They might be pretty subtle, but it would behoove you to learn to identify them and learn how to make them go away. Figure 9-8 shows an outlandish example of this pattern, caused by the screen frequency and angles being set completely wrong.

FIGURE 9-8
Moiré patterns

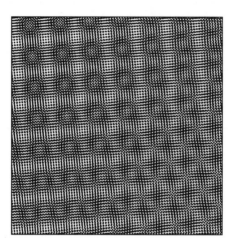

The traditional angles for process colors are: black, 45 degrees; cyan, 75 degrees; magenta, 105 degrees; yellow, 90 degrees. They create a nice rosette, generally free of moiré patterns. However, note that you may not get what you ask for when it comes to angles and screen frequencies. This is a problem between PostScript and the physical limitations of laser printers. For an in-depth discussion, see Chapter 10 on halftoning in *Real World PostScript*.

DOT GAIN
AND PRINTER
CALIBRATION

It's easy to confuse the concepts of dot gain and printer calibration. They both have the same effect. To put it simply, they have to do with why the tint levels you specify in your files are not always what comes out of the imagesetter or off the printing press. For example, you might specify a 40 percent magenta, and your final printed output will look like 60 percent. Don't kick yourself, thinking you typed 60 when you meant 40; remember that the problem could be in three places: dot gain, printer calibration, or your dirty glasses. Let's look at each of these carefully and then explore what can be done about them.

Dot gain. Dot gain occurs while your artwork is actually on the press, and ink is flying about. The primary factors are the amount of ink on the press and the type of paper you're printing on (or, to be more specific, the type of paper your lithographer is printing on). If there's too little ink on the press, your tints may print too light. If there's too much ink or if you're printing onto very absorbent paper, such as newsprint, your tints may print much too dark. A good lithographer can control the ink problem, but the issue of what kind of paper you're printing on must be kept in mind while you're outputting your finished artwork.

Printer calibration. Just to be clear, I'm talking here about image-setter calibration. The idea is this: when the imagesetter's density knob is cranked up to high so the type looks nice and black, and the film processor's chemicals haven't been flushed and replenished in two weeks, your delicate halftoned color separations are going to print less than optimally. All this equipment is so nifty that I sometimes forget that I'm actually dealing with precision instruments designed to be able to produce very high-quality artwork. If you and your service bureau don't understand how to take care of the equipment, the artwork suffers.

Glasses. The third possibility listed above is dirty glasses. In this busy world of contact lenses and corrective eye surgery, you have to stop yourself and ask: why am I wearing these things, anyway? Then remember that if your computer explodes, the shattering glass will harmlessly bounce off those plastic lenses. But remember to keep them clean, or no matter what you do about dot gain and printer calibration, the colors will still look muddy.

ADJUSTING FOR DOT GAIN AND PRINTER CALIBRATION

We live in a less-than-perfect world, and so we require adjustments to compensate for reality. What exactly can we, as Macintosh users, do to ensure high-quality printed output?

First of all, I highly recommend that whoever is doing your imagesetting use a calibration utility such as Kodak's Precision Imagesetter Linearization software or Technical Publishing Service's Color Calibration Software. Proper use of this keeps the image-setter's output relatively consistent on a day-to-day basis. You can then be freed to concentrate on your efforts to compensate for the natural dot gain your art experiences while on the press.

The next thing to do is to make sure the levels in your halftones are set on the light side. Dark tints are notorious for filling in, and if they look too dark on your imagesetter output, they'll be much too dark after they come off the press.

WORKING WITH A SERVICE BUREAU

The existence of service bureaus with imagesetters has mushroomed over the past five years; the phenomenon has grown from a storefront where you could rent a Mac and print on a laser printer to a specialty service where you can send your files to be imageset on a number of medium- and high-end imagesetters. Alongside this growth standard etiquette and rules spoken only in hushed voices (and usually after the customer has left the shop) have developed. In this section I bring these rules out into the open and take you through, step by step, how best to send files to your service bureau, and how to ensure that you'll receive the best quality output from them.

The first thing to remember when dealing with service bureaus is that they don't necessarily know their equipment or what's best for your file any better than you do. That's not to say that they are ignorant louts, but I am of the opinion that good service bureaus are few and far between, and you, the customer, have to be careful and know what you're doing.

The principal subject of this section is sending your Mac files to a service bureau to be imageset. I'll talk first about sending the actual document, and then about sending a PostScript dump of the file. Many of my suggestions may be totally wrong for the way your particular service bureau works, so take what works and leave the rest. Some prefer PostScript dumps, for instance, while others opt for the files themselves.

QUESTIONS
FOR YOUR
SERVICE
BUREAU

Here is a list of a few questions which you may want to ask when shopping for a service bureau.

▶ What imagesetters do they have available, and what resolutions do they imageset at?

▶ Do they have a densitometer?

▶ Do they have dedicated equipment just for film, and do they calibrate it?

▶ Do they have an in-house color-proofing system?

▶ What type of film and processor do they use?

▶ Do they have a replenishing processor, or do they use the same chemicals continually?

▶ Do they inspect their film before it is sent out?

There are no right or wrong answers to any of these. However, asking the questions not only tells you a lot about the service bureau, but also teaches you a lot about the process they're going through to get you your film or RC paper.

You should make decisions about where to run each print job. For example, if a service bureau doesn't calibrate their equipment using a transmission densitometer, you probably don't want to use them for halftoning or color-separation work. If their top resolution is 1270 dpi, you may need to go elsewhere for gray-scale images. You can weigh these items against the cost of the film or paper output, the distance from your office, the friendliness of the staff, and so on.

THE HANDOFF TO THE SERVICE BUREAU

You have two basic choices in transporting your document to a service bureau for imagesetting: sending the file itself, or sending a PostScript dump of the file. Let's be clear right off the bat that I strongly recommend sending a PostScript dump. Why? Mostly because I want to be in control of my document's printing.

When I send the file off to be printed using someone else's system, I don't know whether their fonts are different, whether the text will reflow, whether they'll forget to set up registration marks, or whether they'll print the file at the wrong screen frequency. By sending them a PostScript dump (see "Sending a PostScript Dump," below) you put yourself in the driver's seat: you can control almost every aspect of the print job.

SENDING THE FILE

Though I prefer to send PostScript dumps, I know of service bureaus that prefer to receive the actual file. And the truth is that many people don't want to be responsible for checking all the buttons and specifications necessary to create a PostScript dump. If you find yourself in either of these situations, you'll need to know what to do in order to optimize your chances of success. Let's look at the steps you need to take.

Check your fonts. I can't tell you how important it is to keep track of which fonts you've used and where they are on your disk. Make sure that your service bureau has the same screen fonts as you, and has the downloadable printer fonts that correspond to each and every font you've used in your document. I sometimes send my own screen fonts along with my job to the service bureau because I believe that sometimes screen fonts that are supposed to be the same simply aren't. Either they've gotten corrupted, or it was a different release, or something. But I'd rather be overcareful than have film come back totally wrong.

Chooser and Page Setup. I mentioned that this was possibly just superstition, but I've always found it helpful to make sure I've got a

LaserWriter driver selected in the Chooser and that I've at least checked the Page Setup dialog box once before proceeding to the next step.

Look over your document. Take the extra time to perform a careful perusal of your entire document. If you can, zoom in to 200 percent and scroll over the page methodically. Many problems with printing occur not with the printing at all, but with that one extra word that slipped onto its own line, or the one rule that was "temporarily" placed as a guideline and then never deleted.

Print a proof. If you can print the document on a desktop laser printer, chances are the file will print at your service bureau. That's not a guarantee, but it's usually a pretty good bet. When you print this proof, go over it, too, with a fine-tooth comb. You might have missed something in the on-screen search.

Include your illustrations. If you have imported TIFF or EPS pictures into your document, you may need to include the original files on the disk, along with your document. Check your software manual to see if this applies to you. The idea is to send your service bureau a folder rather than just a file. Give them everything they could ever think of needing, just in case.

CHECKLISTS FOR SENDING MACINTOSH FILES

I find checklists invaluable. Not only do they improve your method by encouraging you to do the appropriate task in the right order, they're a boon to flagging spirits every time you can check an item off the list. Below are examples of checklists I use before sending files to a service bureau.

Fonts

☐ What fonts did you use in your document?

☐ Does your service bureau have your screen fonts? (If not, send them.)

☐ Do they have your printer fonts? (If not, send them.)

Printer Type

☐ Chooser set to LaserWriter or to other appropriate driver?

☐ Page Setup shows appropriate printer?

☐ Printer options checked in Page Setup dialog box? Laser-Writer Options second page dialog box?

Document Check

☐ Check for missing or modified text blocks or pictures.

☐ Check for widows, orphans, runts, loose lines, bad hyphenation, and other typographic problems.

Proof

☐ Print a proof on a laser printer.

☐ Check it carefully. Is it what you want?

Relevant files

☐ Did you include EPS, TIFF, and RIFF files (if your program requires them)?

☐ Did you include the document itself? (Don't laugh, sometimes this is the one thing people *do* forget after a long day.)

Calibration

☐ Check calibration for gray levels.

SENDING A POSTSCRIPT DUMP

It's probably clear that I not only don't trust many service bureaus to do the right thing, but I also don't trust myself to always remember everything I need while standing at the service bureau counter. Because of this, I strongly urge you to use PostScript dumps. A PostScript dump, otherwise known as a "print-to-disk," when performed correctly, almost always ensures a better print, and may be preferred by your service bureau.

In fact, many service bureaus now give big discounts when you bring in PostScript dumps as opposed to the actual files (my neighborhood service bureau cuts five dollars per page off their single-page price). Instead of having to open your file, make sure all the correct fonts are loaded, check all your settings, and then print it, they can take the PostScript dump and send it directly to their imagesetter.

The biggest difference is that you now have the responsibility for making sure your file is perfect for printing. However, this isn't as difficult as it may seem. Let's go through the steps you should take to create the perfect PostScript dump. At the end I'll include a checklist that you can copy or recreate for your own use.

System setup. Make sure you have enough memory on your disk to save the PostScript dump. It will automatically be saved in the same folder as your software (well, actually, sometimes it is arbitrarily saved into the system folder or someplace else, but usually it'll go into the program's folder). PostScript dumps are often not small. They may take up anywhere from 10K to 900K (or larger if you're creating color separations).

Chooser setup. Because you're printing to a PostScript device, you need to have the LaserWriter driver checked in your Chooser. You also need to have Background Printing turned off. It doesn't matter whether you have a PostScript printer hooked up or not.

Page setup. Check your Page Setup dialog box. Read over "Page Setup," above, for more details.

Fonts. You must have the screen font loaded for every typeface you use in your document. If you don't have the screen font for a document, try to get it; without it, you run the risk of having your document print in Courier. In addition, all your line spacing will be messed up, due to a difference in character widths. Note that you don't need the printer font to make this work if your service bureau has it.

Print. The most common mistakes in creating PostScript dumps are made in the Print dialog box. Be careful with the buttons and menus here. If you want multiple copies (not likely for high-resolution output), choose your value here. But if you only want one copy of each page, make sure that you specify "1" here! I've had friends who've accidently gotten 10 copies back from their service bureau simply because they didn't check this carefully. Expensive mistake. Make sure you're aware of the issues covered above in "Other Print Considerations," such as tiling and color separations.

Making the dump. After all that preparation, you are finally ready to make the PostScript dump. The method of creating a PostScript dump depends on the software and LaserWriter driver that you're using. The LaserWriter driver is the file called "LaserWriter" in your system folder. As I said earlier, if it's version 6.0 or higher, it will tell your software to display two buttons: Color/Grayscale and Black & White. If you're running LaserWriter version 7.0 or higher, you also should have buttons labeled "Print" and "PostScript."

To print PostScript to disk from LaserWriter 7.0 or higher, click on the PostScript button, then press OK. The Macintosh asks you where you want the file to be saved and what you want to name it.

Printing PostScript to disk from LaserWriter 6.0 or earlier is a little more difficult. The trick is the "F" and the "K" keys on your keyboard. When you click OK, immediately press the F key on your keyboard. Hold down this key until you see the message "Creating PostScript file." If you start to see messages such as "Preparing Data," you waited too long to press the F key. Cancel, and try again. Some people like to press the mouse button down on OK, then press the F key, then let go of the mouse button. This way they ensure that they'll catch the computer in time.

If you are transferring the PostScript dump to a non-Mac machine before printing, or are printing to a printer that doesn't have Apple's Laser Prep downloaded to it, you should press the K key rather the F key. When you press the K key after clicking OK, the Macintosh includes Apple's Laser Prep information at the beginning of the file. This information is vital to the way your PostScript file runs. However, most service bureaus that use Macintosh computers already have the Laser Prep information downloaded to their printers. If you're unsure of your service bureau, ask them.

A PostScript file generated with LaserWriter 7.0 or higher always has the Laser Prep information included.

e PostScript0 File. I mentioned above where the file would be
ʼed when creating a PostScript dump from LaserWriter 6.0 or
ʼlier, but not what it would be called. The first time you do a
ʼstScript dump, the file is called "PostScript0." The second time,
ʼcalled "PostScript1," and so on. After "PostScript9" the computer
ʼrts over, erasing PostScript0 and replacing it, and so on. I
ʼcommend that after you create your dump, you immediately
ʼange the name to something intelligible, like "Herbie'sBro-
ʼure.ps" (the ".ps" suffix is widely recognized as signifying a Post-
ʼript file, as opposed to some other sort of file).

ʼur service bureau will appreciate you for this one.

System and font setup

☐ Do you have enough room on your disk to save the PostScript
dump?

☐ Do you have the proper screen fonts loaded for the typefaces
that are in your document? EPS files?

☐ Have you hidden or disabled the printer fonts, so they don't
get included in the PS dump?

Chooser and Page Setup

☐ Do you have the LaserWriter or other appropriate driver
selected in the Chooser?

☐ Do you have the proper settings in the Page Setup dialog box?
LaserWriter Options second page dialog box?

Pictures

☐ Do you have all the EPS, TIFF, and RIFF files available?

Print Dialog Box

☐ Are all the proper settings made? Page range? Number of
copies?

☐ Do you want to press the F key or the K key?

MORE SERVICE BUREAU ISSUES

To finish up the chapter, I'm covering a few more issues that you should think about in working with service bureaus: compatibility, enormous file sizes, and including fonts with your PostScript files.

COMPATIBILITY

Fonts change, colors change, everything changes except change itself (if you've heard one cliché, you've heard them all). If you're working with a service bureau regularly, you'll want to make sure that their equipment and system setup are compatible with yours. One way of doing this is for you to use the same files. That is, copy every file from their disk onto yours. This is clearly tedious and never-ending. Another way to go is to perform periodic tests; you can use a test sheet. On this sheet should be the fonts you regularly use, a gray percentage bar, some gray-scale images, and perhaps some line art (just for kicks). The idea is to see whether anything has changed much between your system and the service bureau's. If fonts come out differently, if the tints are off, or if the density is too light or too dark, you can either help them correct the problem or compensate for it yourself.

WHEN YOUR FILE IS TOO BIG

It's easy to make PostScript dumps that are too big to fit onto a floppy. Add a TIFF or an EPS here and there, or even just try to print a large file. Don't fret: there's always a workaround.

First of all, if you're going to work with the Macintosh, you must own a copy of StuffIt and/or Compact Pro. Both of these are shareware programs, which means that you can get them almost anywhere (users' group, dealer, online service), but if you use it more than once, you are honor-bound to send the authors their money (under $25 each). Fortunately for you, I've included a copy of Compact Pro on the Survival Kit disk (see Chapter 11, *Software*).

Some TIFF files can compress as much as 90 percent, although most files only get around 30 to 60 percent smaller. You can also use these programs to break up files into several disks, then join them up again to fit back onto a hard disk.

StuffIt 1.5.1 has become a standard on the Macintosh for compressing files, but Compact Pro can read most StuffIt 1.5.1 files (but not vice versa).

If you're going to be sending lots of large files to your service bureau, I recommend a removable hard disk, such as SyQuest or Bernoulli. Make sure the type you get is compatible with what your service bureau uses. These removables can hold up to 88 megabytes of information. They're also great for backing up your data.

When all else fails, you can use the HDBackup program that ships with Apple's system software. In fact, some people prefer this method. I don't. But I did hear once of someone who did.

TELLING FONTS NOT TO DOWNLOAD

When the Macintosh makes a PostScript dump, it attempts to include any outline printer-font information it can find. For example, if you used Courier in your file and have the Courier printer font in your system folder, the Mac will include that font's information in the file. However, if your service bureau already has the font, you don't need to include it in your PostScript file.

There are two ways to make sure the Mac doesn't include any printer fonts you have floating about. The first option is to move the printer fonts someplace where your software can't find them. This means putting them anywhere but in the system folder, that program's folder, or the folder where you keep your screen fonts. This is another instance where CE Software's DiskTop seems impossible to live without. With it, you can quickly move these files anywhere you want, then return them after you create the print-to-disk file.

However, moving files around is not always the easiest or quickest task. FontStopper is a DA that lets you pick which fonts you want accessible at any given time. When you are ready to create your PostScript dump, you can use FontStopper to make particular printer fonts "disappear." Be aware, though, that as of this writing, FontStopper changes the file type and creator for all those downloadable fonts, and when it changes them back it changes them all to ASPF—the Adobe creator. So once you've used FontStopper, you can't distinguish Adobe from non-Adobe fonts by looking at the creator.

WHEN THINGS GO WORNG

WHAT'S INSIDE

▶ Things are bound to go wrong. The problems you'll encounter are often called anomalies, bugs, or general weirdness.

▶ Problems arise in two areas: software and hardware.

▶ Software weirdness usually has to do with files, programs, or your system not acting like you'd expect it to. Printing problems also fall under the software category.

▶ Hardware weirdness usually has to do with disks, cables, screens, or networks acting strangely.

▶ The best thing to do when confronted with a computer problem is to keep poking at it until you either understand what's going wrong and can fix it, or can work around the situation.

Five years ago, in a galaxy that seems far, far away, I worked at a service bureau that had Macintoshes for rent by the hour. My favorite part of the job was late at night when, I could quietly go about my business without the distraction of other people. My least favorite part of the job was dealing with the strange, twisted, and bizarre problems customers would encounter while attempting to create a newsletter or a book or even something as simple as a one-page resumé. It became a daily occurrence to say, "Wow, that's weird; I've never seen it do *that* before."

In fact, I thought I'd seen it all. Then Valerie Brewster at the *Seattle Weekly* handed me The Strangest Bug I've Ever Seen (see Figure 10-1). What was formatted as a normal column of text came out of the printer as a jumbled scribble; letters were thrown about, ripped in half and strewn randomly across the page.

I knew right then that no matter what I came up against in my desktop publishing experience, it could never be as bad as that bug. And if that could be fixed (it finally was), then any other problem I was faced with could be fixed, too.

FIGURE 10-1
The Strangest Bug
I've Ever Seen

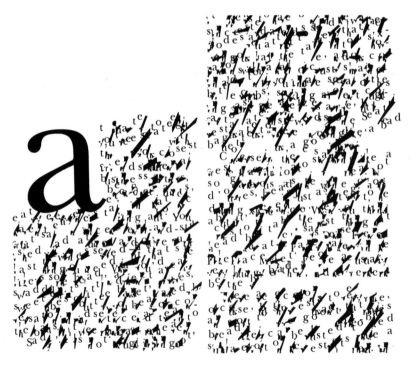

This chapter is dedicated to solving all those problems that come up in the course of a desktop publishing job (usually the night before The 8 A.M. Deadline). I'm breaking the chapter down into two parts: software and hardware. However, before we jump in, let me issue a disclaimer: this chapter is probably not going to answer your questions. There are too many weird things that can go wrong. What I'm really doing here is bringing up some important issues for you to think about when you're stymied, and giving you some options for what to do when you find yourself in Desktop Publishing Hell.

SOFTWARE

Software is the word given to all the intangible parts of your computer. If you can touch it, it's not software. Two examples of software are computer programs (like Microsoft Word or Aldus PageMaker) and the files you create with them. They might be stored on a disk (see "Hardware," later in this chapter), but you can't really touch them, other than smearing the disk with your thumb. Because software is intangible, it's often difficult to figure out what's happening when something goes wrong.

In this section, I'm going to talk about four basic types of software problems and what you can do about them: the computer not doing what you want it to ("I'm sorry, Dave, I'm afraid I can't do that"), your pages or screen not looking like you want them to ("My pages look terrible"), software on your disks getting messed up ("Corruption"), and your pages not printing out from a printer ("Printing Problems").

"I'M SORRY, DAVE, I'M AFRAID I CAN'T DO THAT"

If you've seen the movie *2001: A Space Odyssey*, you've seen a software problem worse than the one Valerie showed me. The way Dave got around the computer not letting him do what he wanted was by killing the computer. Fortunately, you rarely have to do that.

More often, the solution for the computer not doing what you want it to do is to adjust something. Let's look at few examples.

Beeps, bangs, and burps. When the computer beeps at you, it usually means that it can't (or won't) do what you want. This usually happens when you're trying to click someplace where it's not expecting, when the computer runs out of memory, or when it's trying to get your attention. You can adjust the volume of the beep in the Control Panel under the Apple menu. Some people turn the beep off, but I never could figure out why. I figure, if the computer is trying to tell me something, I should at least have the courtesy (and good sense) to listen. If you do turn the beep off, though, the computer flashes the menu bar instead of beeping.

If the beep is a memory problem, and you're operating under MultiFinder (or in System 7, which is always in MultiFinder mode), you may need to quit one or more programs to free up some memory in order to do what you were trying to do. For example, with five megabytes of memory (RAM chips) in my computer, I can usually run FreeHand and QuarkXPress at the same time. However, if I try to open Microsoft Word, too, the computer beeps at me. Not enough memory. I have two choices here: quit one of the programs I'm in, or buy more RAM for my machine.

There's another time when the computer makes interesting sounds at you: when it bombs. If you've used the Macintosh long, you probably know all about system bombs. And believe me, nothing bombs like a Macintosh. The screen can freeze, the cursor can freeze, the computer's speaker can pop and fizzle, bright lines can jump around the screen, and so on. No matter what you were doing when this happens, it is now toast. Burned toast. I hope you saved your work recently, because everything you did since then is probably gone. These sorts of bombs almost never hurt anything on your disk (anything that's been saved), but it's not entirely out of the question for this to happen.

Too many files open. If you do have a lot of memory and you are running MultiFinder, you may find yourself with dialog boxes saying "Too many files open." Sometimes the computer just beeps at you instead (helpful, huh?). The problem here is a setting that tells the operating system how many files you can have open at one time. You can increase this number with programs like Suitcase II,

MasterJuggler, or Bootman (which is included on the Survival Kit disk; see Chapter 11, *Software*). I have mine set to 150. It's that high because various programs have files open "behind the scenes" that you can't see. For example, when you start QuarkXPress, it opens at least one dictionary, a help file, several XTension files, and some filter files. You might have ten or twenty files open before you even open one document.

Can't open printer. As a desktop publisher, I do a lot of printing to my desktop laser printer. Therefore, I'm never a happy camper when I see a dialog box on my screen saying "Can't open printer." Fortunately, this is usually an easy problem to solve. The error usually comes up when you either have no printer selected in the Chooser (see Chapter 9, *Printing*), or when the printer is turned off. If you've checked the Chooser and the printer and you still have the problem, then something weird might have happened to the printer's driver in the System Folder. Make sure that the file called LaserWriter (or whatever driver you're using) is really in the System Folder; if it's corrupted (see "Corruption," later in this chapter), you might need to replace it with a new copy from the original System installation disks (just trash the old file and copy a new one over into your System Folder).

Application needs more memory. Some programs take up lots of memory, and they won't beep at you or tell you when they need more. Some of these programs (we won't name names, because the developers might have fixed these problems by the time you read this) just bomb when they run out of memory. It's not a pleasant thought, since you never know how much memory the program needs at any one time. However, you can often get around this problem. When you select an application in the Finder (click on it once) and select Get Info from the File menu (or type Command-I), you can get some information about that program, including its Suggested Memory Allocation and Application Memory Allocation. The first is what the developers of the program think you should allocate, the second is what you actually allocate. If you work with very large files, you should probably increase the value of the Application Memory Allocation.

For example, Aldus suggests that PageMaker 4.0 be set to a minimum of 1500K (if you don't understand these terms, you should check out Robin Williams' *The Little Mac Book*). However, I usually increase this to 2500K by opening the Get Info dialog box, changing the Application Memory Allocation and then closing the dialog box. You have to do this before you launch the program, but once you do it, the Mac remembers what you've set.

If you aren't running MultiFinder, the only time you'll have this sort of problem is when you don't have enough RAM in your computer (you probably want a minimum of two megabytes of RAM to be efficient in desktop publishing).

MY PAGES LOOK TERRIBLE

Throughout this book, I've tried to give you pointers about how to use the technology to achieve your design goals. However, sometimes no matter how hard you try, your page just doesn't look right. Here are some hints that have helped me over the past few years.

Fonts come out wrong. Don't forget that you have to have the printer fonts for every font used in the document available when you print. That means the fonts you selected, those that were imported, and those that are stuck somewhere in an EPS document. "Available" means that they should be resident in your laser printer or in your System Folder or—if you're using MasterJuggler or Suitcase II—in the same folder as the screen font.

Another very common font problem is font ID conflicts. Each font is assigned a number, as well as a name, by its manufacturer. Unfortunately, sometimes different manufacturers assign the same number to different fonts. And because Macintosh programs often only remember a font's number, the font you ask for may not always be the font you get. If you're experiencing this, you should probably take a good look at Erfert Fenton's *The Macintosh Font Book*; it covers this problem more fully than I can here.

A guy called me the other day with the complaint that the letter spacing and word spacing were all screwed up on his printouts. I said, "Either the text is embedded in a PICT graphic, or you're using a font like New York, Geneva, or Monaco." How was I so sure? Because PICT graphics are notorious for this kind of weirdness (avoid them like the plague!); and those fonts usually get replaced with Times, Helvetica, or Courier but then the letter spacing gets screwed up (see Chapter 3, *Fonts*).

Graphics come out wrong. Possibly the worst nightmare of a desktop publisher is arriving at the local service bureau to pick up 300 pages of film negative output, only to see that every illustration has come out as a low-resolution bitmap. Throwing away a thousand dollars is one way to learn some basics of picture management. Reading this section is another.

When you import a picture into certain programs, they don't actually embed the picture into your document. They only save a low-resolution picture for the screen, while maintaining a link to the original high-resolution image. When you print from that application, it replaces this low-resolution image with the original PostScript or high-resolution graphic. For example, QuarkXPress maintains links to all TIFF and EPS images. PageMaker embeds most EPS images, but only links to TIFF images. Consult your user manual for more information on how your program functions.

As I said back in Chapter 9, *Printing*, the trick is to make sure all the linked files are present and accessible when the file is printed. This usually means that they should be in the same folder as your document, or in the same folder as they were originally imported from. If you send your file to a service bureau, send the linked graphics along, too.

Graphics are patterned. If you're getting plaid or moiré patterns (as described in Chapter 9, *Printing*) from bitmapped images, you have an adjustment to make. If the moiré patterns are the result of combining process colors, there's a good chance the problem is that the screen angle for one or more of the plates is wrong. It's important to know that just because you or your service bureau asks for a particular angle for a color plate doesn't mean you're going to get it. Consult with your service bureau carefully on this issue, and make sure that they're working with an imagesetter that can handle color separations well (like an Optronics ColorSetter or a Linotronic 330 with High Quality Screening).

If you're getting plaid or moiré patterning from a single-color image (like a 1-bit bitmapped image), it's probably scaled so that its resolution does not have an integral relationship to the printer's resolution (i.e., it's not an even multiple). PageMaker has a feature called "magic stretch" that solves this problem. If you're working with another program, you may need to do some calculations. If you scanned the image at 150 dpi, for instance, then reduced it to 74 percent of its original size, you have a 203-dpi scan, which doesn't have an integral relationship to your printer's 300-dpi resolution. Either scale the graphic to 75 percent (resulting in a 200-dpi image), or rescan at a different resolution. Note that what may produce patterns on a 300-dpi laser printer may not produce patterns at all on a higher-resolution imagesetter.

Scans too dark. A good rule of thumb when printing halftoned images is that an area should never be 100 percent black or 100 percent white. The darkest and lightest areas should still have small white or black dots in them when you print on an imagesetter. However, most inexpensive (under $10,000) desktop scanners have a difficult time capturing subtle detail in these highlight and shadow areas, and end up filling them with flat white or black. As I noted in Chapter 7, *Scans & Halftones*, I generally bring scanned images into Adobe Photoshop and adjust the gray levels so that the highlights aren't lighter than 5 or 6 percent black, and so the shadows don't get darker than 93 or 94 percent black (these values depend somewhat on the kind of paper I'm printing on). And don't forget to sharpen those scans, as well, or else they'll probably be too blurry.

CORRUPTION

Given the normal tendencies of a corrupt politician, you'd think that if a file were corrupt, you could bribe it into working. Unfortunately, no matter how much money you stuff into your computer, you'll never get corrupt software to work the way you want it to. Computers aren't interested in money, they're interested in making you frustrated (at least that's how it seems, sometimes).

If you think of software as being words and instructions written in tiny letters on very fragile china plates (a.k.a. magnetic disks), sent back and forth extremely quickly over tiny wires, you can get a sense of how—every now and again—some of those words and instructions can get fouled up. Perhaps there's a chip in the china plate (what techies call a "bad sector"), or perhaps one of those wires between the computer and an external disk drive is slightly loose (what the techies call "bad news"). Whatever it is, these files that get fouled up every now and again are called "corrupted."

Corrupted files have several symptoms. A corrupted System file or application can cause system bombs when you try to work with it. A corrupted font file can corrupt another file which may not be able to be opened or edited or printed, or even saved in a non-corrupted form. Sometimes you can work with a corrupted file for a month before something triggers a problem and the whole file is lost. I don't mean to sound alarmist, but it's a pretty good idea to keep backup copies of your files.

Here are a few more tips for working with corruption in your software.

▶ If you think a font is corrupted, throw it away and load a fresh copy immediately.

▶ If you think that a file is corrupted, you might try to copy everything out of it and paste that information into a new document. Save this new document with a different name from the first.

▶ A corrupt system is the worst. This could include your machine not starting up properly, files disappearing, disks not appearing on your screen at startup, and so on. My first step in this situation is to reach for the Norton Utilities disks. This software has saved more butts than anything else I know of. You may need to reinstall your system (using the system installer that comes with your Macintosh; never just copy a System or Finder file over onto your disk).

▶ If an application is corrupted, it usually just won't launch, or it bombs many more times than is usual. Trash it, and reload a new one (never work from a program's original disk; only work from copies of disks).

PRINTING PROBLEMS

Too often, I get phone calls from my service bureaus saying, "Sorry, your job wouldn't print." Back in the good old days, a service bureau would offer to fix it for you. Now life has gotten busy for them, and they expect you to do the fixing. Here are some tips that I've found to work over the years.

Memory problems. Almost every printer error I see is the result of printer memory problems (called VMerror), and almost all of them can be avoided with a few tricks.

▶ **Reset the printer.** My favorite technique for avoiding memory problems is simply to turn the printer off, wait a few seconds, and turn it back on again. This flushes out any extraneous fonts or PostScript functions that are hogging memory. It's sort of like waking up after a good night's sleep, but different.

   If you're sending a PostScript dump created with the F key (see "Sending a PostScript Dump" in Chapter 9, *Printing*), remember to make sure that the Laser Prep file is download-ed first (resetting the printer gets rid of it). A PostScript dump created with the K key includes the LaserPrep information.

▶ **Use minimum settings.** Using the minimum settings means turning off all the printer options in the Page Setup dialog box, including the LaserWriter Options "second page" dialog box.

▶ **Take care with your fonts.** If you play around with a lot of dif-ferent fonts trying to find one you like, you may inadvertently leave remnants of old fonts lying around your document. For example, a space character may be set in some font that you don't use anywhere else. Nonetheless, the Macintosh must download that font along with every other font you use. This takes up memory that could be used for something else.

▶ **Use Unlimited Downloadable Fonts.** If you must have many fonts on a page, you might want to enable the Unlimited Downloadable Fonts feature in the LaserWriter Options dia-log box under Page Setup.

▶ ***Print fewer pages at a time.*** I have successfully coaxed long documents out of an imagesetter by printing two to 10 pages at a time, rather than trying to get all 500 pages out at once. This is obviously a hassle, but it's better than not getting the job printed at all. Much of the work can be done early by creating multiple PostScript dumps, then queuing them up on a spooler at the service bureau.

▶ ***Remove enormous graphics.*** One of the great promises of desktop publishing was that I could print out an entire page with every graphic and text block perfectly placed. Remember that promises are often broken. Case in point: large graphics (or even small graphics) sometimes choke the printer. These graphics often will print all by themselves, but when placed on a page, they become the chicken bone that killed the giant. Yes, using every trick possible you might get the page out, but is it worth the time? Perhaps it's more efficient to just let your printer or stripper handle that graphic. Or, God forbid, just hot-wax that puppy and paste it down yourself.

PostScript problems. There are some PostScript problems that aren't memory-related, though they're rare. One is the infamous limitcheck error. Another is the undefined command error. These are significantly harder to track down and fix. However, here are a few things you can try.

▶ ***Save as.*** Logically, saving your document under a different name doesn't make any sense, but it does work sometimes.

▶ ***Selective printing.*** You can try to pinpoint what page element is causing the error by printing only certain parts of the page. For example, remove all the graphics from a stubborn page; if the page prints, chances are that one of the graphic images is at fault.

   If the page still doesn't print without graphics, try taking out a text box at a time, or changing the fonts you used. If you're printing color separations, try printing one color at a time.

▶ ***Simplify the graphic.*** Many limitcheck errors come from a curve with hundreds of points on it, or a very large graphic with a very large curve in it, this could easily crash your print job. Try raising the flatness of that curve, or breaking it up into smaller paths. The flatness of a curve determines how hard the printer has to calculate to create a smooth curve. Increasing the flatness of a complex curve in FreeHand or Illustrator to a value of 3 or 4 (see your manual on how to do this) can not only help the file print, but it often speeds up printing time considerably.

▶ *Shrink the page size.* For technical reasons I don't need to get into here, some pages avoid PostScript errors when printed at a smaller size. You can use the Reduce or Enlarge setting in the Page Setup dialog box to print the page at 25 or 50 percent of size. Of course, this will rarely help you in the long run. This method is only for really complex graphics or pages.

▶ *Reimport.* If the problem turns out to be a graphic you've imported, you might try reimporting it. Even better, if the image is in the PICT format, convert it into a better format, like TIFF (for bitmaps) or EPS (for object-oriented graphics). Then reimport it.

▶ *md dict.* The "md dict" is the collection of procedures in the Laser Prep file. When you print a file directly from within the program, Apple's LaserWriter driver checks to see if the md dict is present. If it isn't, it gets downloaded automatically. However, if you're sending PostScript dumps to a printer, you may end up with undefined command errors because the printer can't find the proper procedure. The easiest way to download the LaserPrep information is to print a single blank page from almost any Macintosh application (not Aldus PageMaker; it doesn't usually use the Laser Prep).

Big ugly white gaps appear between colors. You've output your four-color separations and sent the file off to your lithographer. A few days later you show up for the press check and you see, much to your surprise, big ugly white gaps appearing between each of the colors. What happened? You forgot about traps. It's easy to do, believe us. The remedy? Go read the section on trapping in Chapter 8, *Color*, and redo your negatives.

Wrong screen frequency. If you can't set your own halftone screen frequency using your software, you're probably stuck with the default for your printer. Most (if not all) desktop laser printers are set to 53 lines per inch. Many imagesetters default to 120 or 150 lines per inch. If you can set the halftone screen frequency (you can in PageMaker and QuarkXPress), you should. Note that this is not a function your service bureau can easily change if you provide a PostScript dump.

Registration problems. Imagine the Rockettes, kicking their legs to chorus line stardom in perfect synchronization. Then imagine the woman at one end having no sense of rhythm, kicking totally out of sync with the others. This is what happens when one color plate is misregistered with the others. When a sheet of paper is rushed through a printing press and four colors are speedily applied to it, there is bound to be some misregistration—sometimes up to a point or two. However, you can help matters considerably by making sure that your film is as consistent as possible.

Whenever I am told that a job printed great "except for one plate that was off register," I immediately ask if that plate was imageset at a different time than the others. The answer is almost always yes. I realize that it's expensive and time-consuming to print four new plates every time you want to make a change to a page, but it is a fact of desktop life that you can almost never get proper registration when you re-imageset a single plate. Why? The weather, film stretch, alignment of the stars…all sorts of reasons contribute to this massive hassle.

HARDWARE

No discussion of weirdness would be complete without a foray into hardware problems. If software is intangible, then hardware is everything that you can actually touch (and—just for the sake of reference—"wetware" is the affectionate term for the gray mushy stuff in your head). For example, the screen, cables, disks, and computer are all hardware. Let's take a look at where some hardware problems might show their heads.

DISKS

The most common hardware problem has to do with the disks we store information on. That might be an internal or external hard disk, a removable disk (like a SyQuest or Bernoulli system), or a floppy disk (which, on the Macintosh, isn't really that floppy). All of these disks are what's called "magnetic media"; there are little particles jam-packed onto the disk which can retain magnetic charges for a long time. The magnetic charges "remember" your information (it's like flying in an airplane: you don't have to know the physics, just believe that it works).

Disks can have several things go wrong with them. First, disks wear out. If you read and write material to the same disk for years, it may wear out. Second, disks can be defective in areas. Sections of the disk (called sectors) can wear out faster than others or just start out bad, fouling up the information written there.

Third, disks can be destroyed easily. If you drop a SyQuest cartridge out your window, it'll probably die. On the other hand, I play frisbee with floppy disks and they usually still work. However, if you place a floppy disk on top of a big speaker, it may die (speakers have magnets in them, which confuse the magnetic particles on the disk). If you open your hard drive to see what's inside and dust gets in, the dust particles could be dragged across the surface of the disk and wipe out information.

Disks are fragile pieces of work and, as Willie Loman's wife is fond of saying, "Attention must be paid." Save often, keep backups, and have a copy of Norton Utilities (or some other disk-saving software) around. If something bad does happen to a disk, I usually try to get the information off of it as quickly as possible. If it's a floppy disk, I throw it out as soon as I can. If it's something more expensive, I back up the whole thing and run some disk doctoring software on it (such as Norton Utilities).

CABLES AND WIRES

Cables and wires are the freeways of a computer system. Information is passed back and forth at extremely high speeds. Imagine a freeway with a big crack in it, or a gap between the roadway and the off ramp. Cars would be flying all over the place, right? Similarly, your cables must be in good shape, and not just partially plugged in.

There are two other strange things that can go on with cables. One is called SCSI Voodoo, the other is Black Magic Networking.

SCSI Voodoo. Most hard drives and peripherals (like scanners) are connected through SCSI cables (usually pronounced "scuzzy," though sometimes it's called "sexy"). The cables are plugged into SCSI ports. If you're using SCSI, read the manuals carefully. However, even then strange things can occur. For example, one hard drive might not show up on your desktop until you rearrange the order in which your peripherals are linked. Or, sometimes just switching two cables might change something. Often, neither of these things makes any rational sense (at least not to anyone other than a networking specialist); it just works. That's why I call it voodoo.

Black Magic Networking. Many networks have similar problems. Laser printers don't show up in the Chooser dialog box, servers appear and disappear randomly, and files get corrupted in transit over network lines. I have to admit that I know very little about this area. Once, in the middle of a particularly bad day, I kept thinking, "If only I knew a secret incantation I could say that would make this all work!" I realized that some bozo had kicked out one of the AppleTalk connectors.

COMPUTERS

The last area I'll talk about in this chapter is general computer problems that every now and again rear their ugly heads. Sometimes the weirdest things are the easiest to fix. Other times you'll just have to haul your computer down to the service station.

For example, the simplest hardware problem I've troubleshot was for the person who kept complaining that the colors on her screen were too dark. I was about to tell her to take it in for servicing, when I discovered that she had just turned the brightness control down on her monitor.

If your computer or laser printer is running out of memory too often (can't open enough applications, or print jobs keep dying unexpectedly), think about adding more memory. At the time of this writing, memory is pretty inexpensive, and you can often install it yourself.

JUST KEEP POKING

Let's take a quick test of what you've learned. What do you do when the computer does something that you don't understand or think that you should be able to do?

- *Give up immediately.* If this is your answer, go back and read this chapter again. Defeatists rarely succeed in this business.

- *Call a consultant.* If you're response has the word "consultant in it" I sure hope you've got a lot of money to burn!

- *Try to understand the problem.* This is a good start, but concentrating on what's wrong can lead to depression and existential angst.

- *Find a workaround.* This is the best answer to the question.

The lesson of this chapter is Just Keep Poking. If you work with the Macintosh long enough, you're sure to come across some strange problems that seem insoluble. But remember that if you're creative with your solutions, you can almost always either fix the problem or find a way around it. Good luck!

CHAPTER 11
SOFTWARE

WHAT'S INSIDE

▶ Computer programs are the primary tools with which you do your job.

▶ When considering what software to buy, you need to ask yourself, "What software best suits my needs?"

▶ Just having a basic page-layout program is good, but having backup utilities and desk accessories is even better.

▶ The enclosed Survival Kit disk is chock full o' great software that you can use. However, some of it is shareware, and if you use it regularly, you are honor-bound to send the author a small fee.

Who was it that said, "Desktop publishers cannot survive on fonts and file formats alone"? These words of wisdom bring us to the last chapter of this book, where we take a look at the real tools of the trade: computer software. If graphic file formats, typefaces, halftones, and color models are the vegetables and beans, then computer programs make up the kitchen in which you prepare your gourmet meal. In this book I've focused primarily on the ingredients of the meal, but this chapter is dedicated to the tools of the kitchen.

I've broken this chapter down into three basic sections. The first covers general software concerns: what you should think about when considering software. The second section outlines what I consider to be important computer software for desktop publishing on the Macintosh. The third section describes everything that's on the Survival Kit disk.

WHEN CONSIDERING SOFTWARE

When I was a kid, we *really* had it tough. Back in the good ol' days of Macintosh desktop publishing, the only tools we had were MacPaint, MacDraw, and MacWrite. We printed everything on an ImageWriter (a 72-dpi dot-matrix printer). And, although we knew that our artwork looked like crud, we masked this by saying it was our style.

Then PageMaker and PostScript came along and made things complicated. Soon a slew of programs flooded the market, until we got what we have today: marketing mania. Everybody is so caught up in "My software's bigger than yours" that almost no one is asking the basic question: "What software best suits my needs?"

In this section, I'm going to talk about three basic types of software: page-layout, illustration, and painting. There are many more areas than these, of course; but this is a book on desktop publishing, so I'll limit myself. Nonetheless, I urge you to ask questions similar to the ones I'll pose here when you're considering a word-processing, telecommunications, spreadsheet, or any other kind of program.

Page layout. The most basic desktop publishing software is the page-layout package, where you place text and graphics together on a page. The most common page-layout programs on the Macintosh are Aldus PageMaker and QuarkXPress (those of you who've read another book of mine, *The QuarkXPress Book*, know my particular bias). However, there are many more programs to choose from, including Publish It Easy, RagTime, FrameMaker, Ventura Publisher, and DesignStudio.

These are great programs for particular tasks and for particular people. However, describing each of them, explaining how it might be right for you, could easily fill another whole book. Instead, let's look at two basic points to consider when looking at page-layout programs.

First, how much power do you need "under the hood"? There's no need for an administrative assistant who's been asked to create flyers for the company picnics to use QuarkXPress or Ventura Publisher. That's like giving a Ferrari to someone to who's just driving down to the store; they can use it, but they could also do as good a job with a solid Honda.

Second, what sorts of tools do you need in the program? If you're creating a math textbook, you had better be able to typeset equations easily (as you can in FrameMaker). If you're creating a technical manual that needs an extensive cross-referenced index, you had better be great at doing that sort of thing by hand, or have a tool (like PageMaker) that helps you. If you don't have a paint or illustration program, you might consider a program that has some of that functionality built in (for example, Publish it Easy). One of my favorite programs is RagTime, because it has so many different tools in it that no other program does, and yet is geared toward an office market.

Illustration. As I said back in Chapter 2, *Graphic File Formats*, illustration programs create object-oriented graphic files. Typical examples of illustration programs are Adobe Illustrator, Aldus FreeHand, Canvas, and MacDraw. Again, it's important to look at how much power you really need and what sort of tools you need in a program. If you aren't printing to a PostScript printer, then the EPSF files that come out of Illustrator and FreeHand aren't going to help you much. And if you need to handle a lot of text in your illustrations, you may need a program with a search-and-replace feature or a spelling checker (like Canvas 3.0).

Paint. Paint programs create and modify bitmapped images, such as those in the PNTG and TIFF file formats. These might be scans, screen captures, or synthetic images. There are many different types of paint programs, including Adobe Photoshop, Enhance, Color-Studio, and DeskPaint. I have a particular bias here towards Photoshop and DeskPaint, for two different reasons. First, Photoshop does almost everything I could ever want in a paint program. It can even import and manipulate many EPSF pictures. Second, DeskPaint is amazing because it's a great paint program in the form of a desk accessory. Because DeskPaint doesn't handle complicated image manipulation or large bitmapped images very well, I use it primarily as a tool for screen shots and quick changes on 72-dpi black-and-white or color images.

IMPORTANT COMMERCIAL SOFTWARE

Beyond the high-end non-stick frying pans and woks of our desktop publishing kitchen are the whisks, spatulas, and wooden spoons. Or, for those of you in the entertainment business: the lead singers are nothing without their backup band. In this section, I'm going to cover some of the important members of "the backup band" that make our life so much sweeter.

MasterJuggler or Suitcase II. Handling fonts and desk accessories is a constant hassle. Unless you only have ten fonts and six desk accessories that you always use and never change, you will want to have a font and DA management utility like MasterJuggler or Suitcase II. These are both DAs that let you load or unload (access and unaccess) fonts and DAs as you need to. They have other features as well, like managing sounds, and resolving font conflicts. My personal favorite is MasterJuggler (see Figure 11-1). It's significantly more intuitive and easy to use, plus it has a great application-switching function that I couldn't live without. Most people buy Suitcase II, though, because they've got better marketing. Go figure.

FIGURE 11-1
MasterJuggler

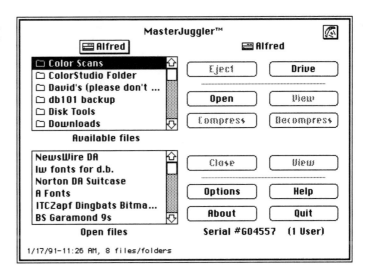

ATM. I talked about Adobe Type Manager (ATM) and type rendering back in Chapter 3, *Fonts*. The concept, in a nutshell, is that ATM uses the outline printer fonts to create screen fonts as you type. When you change to a particular type size, ATM generates the best-looking screen fonts it can for you. If you don't use a PostScript printer, ATM is an absolute must. With it, you can get the highest-quality type at any size. If you work with headline-size type or need to do any precision type placement, you'll want to use rendered type, too.

QuicKeys. I'm not quite sure how I lived without CE Software's QuicKeys. I guess I was just too young to know any better. QuicKeys is a macro-making utility. Macros are shortcuts that you can access at a keystroke. For example, I can close the frontmost window, open desk accessories, or type my address by typing a keystroke that I've assigned (usually something like Control-L). There are several other macro-making utilities on the market, including Tempo II and

Macro Maker (which comes free from Apple), but QuicKeys is my favorite for general use.

DiskTop. DiskTop is another great piece of software from CE Software that has made my life much better. It's a desk accessory that performs many of the Finder's functions. For example, I can move, copy, delete, rename, or find files quickly, without leaving the application that I'm working in. I can also change a file's type and creator, and add notes to it. More programs of this kind are showing up on the scene, but DiskTop is tried and true for me.

Checklist. Whereas ElseWare's Checklist 1.0 was shareware and aimed primarily at the PageMaker user, their version 2.0 is a commercial application and is helpful to almost anybody. Checklist is amazing at handling fonts, PostScript files, and PageMaker documents. It catches problems in your files such as missing fonts and graphics and non-standard print settings (see Figure 11-2). If you work at a service bureau, you will fall to your knees and thank the heavens that Checklist was created. If you work with a service bureau, you may not have such a strong reaction, but I think you'll be tempted to write a thank-you letter to the programmers.

More DAs and CDEVs. No discussion of important software could be complete without including Boomerang and LaserStatus.

FIGURE 11-2
Checklist

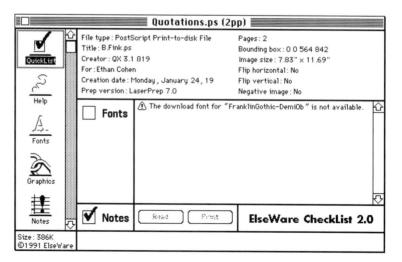

Boomerang, a CDEV (control panel device), adds features to your Save and Open dialog boxes. For example, you can jump to the last folder you were in or assign a keystroke to a particular file that you often use. It's become central to how I work on the Mac. Boomerang used to be shareware, but now there's a newer version (Super Boomerang) that is commercial software.

CE Software has several other precious utilities, including the LaserStatus DA, which lets you download fonts and PostScript files to a printer without having to switch to another program. It can also retrieve information about your printer's status (busy, idle, what fonts are loaded, and so on) or reset it without your having to walk over to the printer.

THE DISK

I always read the last line of a book first, just to make sure it doesn't say, "And they lived happily ever after." If you've done that with this book, you've probably noticed a disk hiding inside the back cover. This is the Survival Kit disk. Instead of giving you a bandage, a snake-bite kit, and four strike-anywhere matches, I've included over 1.6 megabytes of software aimed directly at making you a more efficient desktop publisher. There's so much software that you'll need a hard disk drive to copy it all onto. If you don't have a hard disk drive, get one soon. There's very little you can do as a desktop publisher these days without one.

In this section, I'm going to tell you everything you need to know about the disk and what's on it. You could just jump in and start using the software, but I think you'll get more out of it if you read the rest of this chapter first.

GETTING
STARTED

Absolutely the first thing you should do with the Survival Kit disk is lock it and make a copy of it. Lock it so that you don't accidently erase anything off it, or spread a virus onto the disk. You can lock it by moving the little plastic square in the upper right corner of the disk with your fingernail so that you can see through the hole. You should copy the disk for archival purposes. That is, if your computer explodes while this disk is in it, you'll have a copy of it somewhere else (then all you'll need is a new computer).

The second thing you should do is double-click on the Read Me First file on the disk. If nothing happens or you get a dialog box saying it couldn't find the application to open, then you probably don't have a copy of TeachText on your hard disk. Almost everyone who has a Macintosh has TeachText on their computer somewhere, even if they don't know about it. If you're one of the few who don't, you can find it on your original Apple system disks.

The primary message in the Read Me First file is that you need to have the Compact Pro software in order to open all the other files on the disk. Fortunately, I've included a copy of Compact Pro for you. Simply double-click on the file that is labelled Compact Pro.sea. The suffix ".sea" means "self-extracting archive." This tells you that when you double-click on it, it uncompresses itself onto another disk (wherever you tell it to go).

You really should read the documentation that comes with Compact Pro so that you can get the most out of it. However, just to get you started, I'll tell you how to uncompress the files on the disk.

1. Start Compact Pro. You can do this by double-clicking on either the program itself, or on any one of the compressed files on the Survival Kit disk.

2. If you didn't double-click on one of the compressed files, then you'll need to open one now. Select Open from the File menu, and select one of the files from the disk.

3. Click on the files you want to extract (decompress), or type Command-A to select all of them.

4. Select Extract from the Archive menu, or type Command-E. Tell Compact Pro where to save those files, and click OK.

That's all there is to it!

IMPORTANT
NOTES

The software that's on the disk is either freeware, shareware, or commercial. I'll tell you what's what in the software descriptions later in this chapter.

Freeware means that you can use it, copy it, give it to friends, or feed it to your pet iguana without a charge. It's free.

Shareware means that you can use it just like freeware, but if you like it and use it regularly, you are honor-bound to pay the author of the shareware (not me) whatever he or she has asked for it. This is usually a very small amount, between one and thirty dollars, and is always reasonable. The programmer put in a lot of time writing this software, and should be paid for it if you use it. The programmers aren't getting any money from the purchase of this book; but they've agreed to let me put their software on this disk in hopes that you'll like it and send them some money.

You can use the commercial software on this disk with no additional payment, but you shouldn't give it to friends or upload it to bulletin board systems, and so on.

My liability. All of this software is provided to you on an "as-is" basis. That means if you don't like it, if it doesn't work, or if it messes something up for you, I cannot take responsibility for it. The same goes for Peachpit Press. I have, however, taken every precaution to ensure that almost nothing can go wrong. There may be some software here that doesn't work on your machine. For example, some of this software may not work fully under System 7. There are so many different system configurations out there that I cannot predict how this software will work on your machine. You'll just have to try it.

Problems. If you have problems with any of the software, make sure you've taken all these steps.

▶ Read the section describing each piece of software.

▶ Look for ReadMe files, help files, or documentation that comes with the disk.

▶ Look for on-line documentation when you're running the program. This might be a Help button, or a message in the About... dialog box (usually found on the Apple menu).

Copyright. All of the software on the Survival Kit disk is copyrighted by an author. Ultimately, they have the rights to the software. You usually can't change anything about the software without their permission, or distribute the software without proper documentation. Check with the documentation that's on the disk or in an online help dialog box for more information.

CLIP ART

Clip art pictures are images that you can use in your documents. I've included ten EPSF images, ten PNTG (Paint) images, and a grayscale 8-bit TIFF image (see Chapter 2, *Graphic File Formats*).

3G Graphics. 3G Graphics is known as the creator of some of the best EPSF clip art available. I've included eight of its high-quality art files in the Clip Art compressed file. Each file is saved in the Illustrator 1.1 format. This means that you can open and modify the artwork with Adobe Illustrator or Aldus FreeHand. You can view the images by importing them into a page-layout program such as PageMaker or QuarkXPress.

This clip art is commercial software, for your own use. You can get more information about 3G Graphics at 3G Graphics, Inc., 11410 N.E. 124th, Suite 6155, Kirkland, WA 98034. Toll-free phone: (800) 456-0234 (U.S. only), or (206) 367-9321.

T/Maker. T/Maker is very well known for its Paint and EPSF clip art on both the Macintosh and PC platforms. Here, I've included twelve images: two EPSF and ten Paint images. Each of these images can be imported into a page-layout program, or opened using a paint or illustration program.

This clip art is also commercial software, for your own use. You can get more information about T/Maker at T/Maker, Inc., 1390 Villa Street, Mountain View, CA 94041. Phone: (415) 962-0195; fax: (415) 962-0201.

FONTS

There's no such thing as too many fonts! Here are two more fonts for your library: Hardwood™ and Encyclofont.

Hardwood. Hardwood is a Type 1 PostScript font from LetterPerfect. It can be used as either a text or headline typeface, and is ATM-compatible. This is commercial software, and shouldn't be given away. You can get more information about LetterPerfect and its

fonts (as well as information about custom typefaces) by writing to
LetterPerfect, 6606 Soundview Drive, Gig Harbor, WA 98335. Phone:
(206) 851-5158.

Encyclofont. The Encyclofont was created by Deke McClelland and
Craig Danuloff for use in their book, *Encyclopedia Macintosh*. It
contains symbols for the most common Macintosh keyboard and
mouse commands, such as Command, Option, Shift, Control,
"click" and "click and drag." It's a Type 3 font generated with
KeyMaster, from Altsys.

   This font is freeware.

SOFTWARE

Here are twelve of the most helpful utilities, DAs, and CDEVs
(control panel devices) for desktop publishers that I could find .
Each of them is in a compressed Compact Pro file (that's how I
could get so much information on one disk).

Compact Pro. I talked a little about Compact Pro earlier in this
chapter. It's the key to the Survival Disk files, because you need it to
uncompress them. However, Compact Pro is useful for more than
that. Compact Pro can compress almost any file down to 10 to 60
percent of its original size (different files compact differently). If
you're running out of space on your disk, you can archive some files.
You can also segment large files into smaller ones, and perform a
variety of other tasks. As I said earlier, to use Compact Pro, you must
first double-click on the self-extracting archive (.sea file) that's on
the Survival Kit disk, and then direct the program to the folder
where you want to save the uncompressed version of Compact Pro.

   Compact Pro is shareware. If you find yourself using it regularly,
please send $25 to Bill Goodman at 109 Davis Avenue, Brookline,
MA 02146. The author is also available via electronic mail at
CompuServe 71101,204.

Add/Strip. Add/Strip is a great utility for massaging text files that are
coming from or going to PCs and other types of computers. It's also
great for processing text files that are going to stay on the Macintosh. I recommend a quick read of the text file that comes with

Add/Strip, and a more thorough read of the on-line documentation (found in the About... item on the Apple menu).

Add/Strip is shareware. If you find yourself using it regularly, please send $25 to Jon Wind, 2374 Hillwood Drive, Maplewood, MN 55119. The author is also available via electronic mail at CompuServe 70167,3444, Genie: JPWIND, MCI Mail: J.WIND, and America Online: JWIND.

Blender. If you use Aldus FreeHand or Adobe Illustrator (or any other program) to create blends from one process color to another, you'll want to use Blender. This easy-to-use desk accessory (DA) tells you how many steps you should use in your blend, depending on the colors, the resolution of the printer, and the screen frequency of the tints. It even tells you how long you should make the blend to avoid banding problems. Instructions are all online (click the Help button).

Blender is shareware. If you find yourself using it regularly, please send between $1 and $5 to Rick Johnson, Graffix, 2216 Allen Lane, Waukesha, WI 53186. The author is also available by electronic mail at Genie: RICK.JOHNSON, CompuServe: 75135,1740 and America Online: Guntherdog.

Bootman. Back in Chapter 10, *When Things Go Worng*, I noted that you might need Bootman to raise the number of files that you can have open at one time. Bootman has two other functions as well: changing the system heap size and the maximum number of operating system events. The concept of system heap is too complex to get into here, but Bill Steinberg (the author of Bootman) has included great documentation in the program. Operating system events are things like keystrokes and mouse clicks. If you find that you're typing so fast that your computer can't keep up with you, raising the number of allowable system events might help.

Bootman is freeware. Use it, give it away, but remember that the author still holds the copyright on the software (so you can't sell it or change it). The author can be reached by electronic mail at CompuServe: 76703,1027, AppleLink: X0542, and America Online: BillS NYC.

MiniConversion. If you've ever been stumped when faced with converting picas to feet, or inches to centimeters, MiniConversion is here to help. This desk accessory gives you many conversion options, including both PostScript and traditional points and picas, inches, miles, and kilometers. This program is shareware (between $1 and $5), and was written by the same person who created Blender, listed above.

miniWRITER. MiniWRITER is an entire word-processing text editor in a desk accessory. I use this constantly for jotting down and printing notes, quickly browsing through text files, and performing search-and-replace operations. It even performs many of the basic functions of Add/Strip (see above), such as adding or stripping curly quotes and other non-standard ASCII characters. You don't want to use miniWRITER for large text files (if the file is too large, mini-WRITER may not even open it), but for anything between a small note and a couple of pages, this is the cat's pajamas.

MiniWRITER is shareware. If you find yourself using it regularly, please send $12 to Maitreya Design, P.O. Box 12085, Eugene, OR 97440.

PixelFlipper. Efficiency! Anyone who knows me well knows that I aim for efficiency. Reaching for the mouse when I'm on a roll, or typing three extra keystrokes can drive me crazy! PixelFlipper is a great efficiency tool: it lets you switch between screen color depths with a keystroke and mouse click. For example, if you want to switch from 8-bit color mode to 1-bit black-and-white mode, you can hold down a customizable key combination (mine's Command and Control) and click on the screen somewhere. A pop-up menu appears, and you can select the color you want.

PixelFlipper is shareware. If you find yourself using it regularly, please send $10 to Chris Sanchez, 630 Barr Drive, Ames, IA 50010. The author is also available by electronic mail at CompuServe: 76547,1254, and America Online: BBun.

PopChar. Trying to find the correct key combination for a ligature or a copyright mark can be frustrating if your memory is as short as mine. After frequent trips to the Key Caps desk accessory, PopChar is a relief. It's a CDEV (you put it in your System Folder) that can pop up a dialog box showing all of the characters in any font that you're currently using, at the click of a mouse. Move the mouse over the character you want, and PopChar shows you what the keystroke should be.

PopChar is freeware, but the author reserves all rights to it, so don't go and try to sell it or change it outside what's allowed in the documentation. You can contact the author at the following address: Günther Blaschek, Petzoldstrasse. 31, A–4020 Linz, Austria. He can also be reached via electronic mail at Bitnet: K331671@ AEARN or Internet: gue@soft.uni-linz.ac.at.

SmartKeys. If you've been reading this book chapter by chapter, then you know that you should almost never type two spaces in a row on a Macintosh, and you should use em dashes instead of two hyphens (see Chapter 4, *Word Processing*). SmartKeys is here to help you in your transition from the world of typewriters to the world of desktop publishing. It's a CDEV that has several functions. Among other things, it can prevent you from typing two spaces in a row (it tells the Mac to ignore any more than one space), it can automatically replace double hyphens with em dashes, and can insert ligatures wherever you type "fi" or "fl." It even fixes the common typing mistake where you hit the Shift-period key when typing "a.m." (otherwise you'd get "a<m<"). Another nice feature of SmartKeys is that you can set most of the functions not to work in certain applications. For example, if you don't want curly quotes in a telecommunications program, you can tell SmartKeys not to function in that program.

SmartKeys is freeware, but the author retains all copyrights. Bug reports and other comments/questions can be sent to the author at the following address: Maurice Volaski, 173 Princeton Avenue, Apartment #2, Amherst, NY 14226-5006. Electronic mail can be sent via the Internet to volaski@contra.med.buffalo.edu.

theFONDler. These next two programs were written by Jim Lewis at Golden State Graphics, and are designed to make life with fonts as pleasant as possible. In Chapter 3, *Fonts*, I wrote at some length about the complicated world of fonts. TheFONDler not only helps you organize your font collection by providing in-depth information about each font, but it comes with extensive documentation about fonts, harmonizing suitcases, and how to handle them (Jim's had lots of experience in this field).

TheFONDler is shareware. If you find yourself using it regularly, please send $25 to Jim Lewis at Golden State Graphics, 2137 Candis Avenue, Santa Ana, CA 92706. The author can also be reached by electronic mail on CompuServe: 71650,2373 or America Online: JimXLewis.

theTypeBook. I don't know about you, but I can't always remember what all my fonts look like. I know the basics, like Palatino has serifs and Futura doesn't, but when I really want to compare typefaces, I need specimen sheets. That's where theTypeBook comes in. This utility can create four different specimen (spec) sheets: Sample Layout, Key Caps Table, Character Set, and Line Showings. The included documentation describes each of these fully, and tells you how to customize the layouts to suit your needs.

TheTypeBook is freeware (though I don't think the author would turn down a donation for his time and effort). Jim can be reached at the address listed above.

Unity. Unity is perhaps the simplest utility on the Survival Kit disk. Its whole purpose in life is to concatenate (bring together) text files. Let's say that you have six separate text files that you wish were all in one file. You could open the first in a word-processing program (or with miniWRITER; see above), select all the text, copy it, then open the second, paste the first file's text into it, and so on. Or, you could use Unity.

Unity is shareware. If you find yourself using it regularly, please send $5 to Michael O'Rourke, 5663-201 Columbia Road, Columbia, MD 21044. The author can also be reached by electronic mail on the Internet at mko@sundec.umd.edu.

WHERE TO GET MORE

The clip art, fonts, and software on the Survival Kit disk barely scratch the surface of freeware and shareware software that is available. You can do three things to find more software like this.

► Join a user's group. Macintosh users' groups have sprung up all over the world. Many of them have software libraries full of goodies. To find out where your nearest user's group is, call Apple at (800) 538-9696 and ask for extension 500.

► Get a modem and join an online service (electronic bulletin board system, or BBS). As you've probably noticed in reading the descriptions of the Survival Kit disk software, almost everybody who's anybody is connected to an online service. The most popular are CompuServe and America Online, which anyone can get an account on (as long as you pay for it). Both of these have lots of software available, as well as electronic mail and online forums for chatting with other folks around the world.

If you're connected to Apple in some way (as a developer, dealer, etc.), you can buy time on AppleLink. If you're connected to a large computer corporation or educational institution, you can probably get an account on the Internet or Bitnet.

► Find a shareware distributor. There are several large and many small distributors of shareware and freeware around. For example, Educorp will send you a disk full of software for six or seven dollars. Don't forget that what's on the disk is often shareware, and you may have to pay those fees over and above what the disk costs you (these services charge for the disks to cover their overhead).

Once you've found sources for the software, the only thing left for you to do is figure out what software is worth having. The best way to do this is to talk to friends and colleagues at users' group meetings, or on the online services. Don't be shy; in this wild desktop-publishing jungle, we've all got to stick together.

INDEX & GLOSSARY

Cut. *See* Clipboard

D

Deep bitmapped image 11. *A bitmapped images that has a pixel depth of two or more bits.*

Densitometer 123. *See also* Printing. *A tool that measures the density of black. Also often used to measure gray values.*

Descenders. *See* Ascenders and descenders.

DeskPaint 152

Desktop color. *See* Color

Desktop publishing. *Creating artwork and documents using desktop computers.*

Dialog boxes 3

Digitize. *Converting artwork or lettering into an electronic form by either scanning it or recreating it on the computer.*

Dingbats. *See* Special characters

Discretionary hyphen. *A hyphen that tells the computer where to break a word if it needs to. When the word isn't broken, the hyphen is invisible. Also called a "dischy."*

Disks 146

DiskTop 15, 21, 131, 154

Dithering 16. *Simulating grays or colors by using patterns of dots.*

Dot gain 120–122. *The darkening of a tint due to ink spread or poor calibration. In printing, this is often very apparent on uncoated paper.*

Dots per inch 10. *See also* Resolution

Dots 80. *See also* Halftones

Drop caps. *Inital letters in a paragraph that are enlarged and indented into the text beneath them.*

Duotone. *A gray-scale image that is printed with two colors, often black and a spot color.*

E

Ellipsis 46. *A series of three dots that indicate an ommision or a pause in a sentence.*

Elseware 154

Em dash 41. *A dash the length of an em space.*

Em space 41, 56. *A space that is usually as long as the type size. For example, an em space in 14-point text is 14 points long.*

Emphasis 30, 41, 54

Emulsion. *See* Printing. *Light-sensitive chemicals on one side of film or RC paper.*

En dash 41–42

En space. *Half the length of an em space.*

Encylofont 158–159

EPSF 8, 16–18, 21, 125, 139. *Encapsulated PostScript (EPSF) is a form of PostScript that can be imported into other programs. It often has a low-resolution embedded preview image.*

Extended face. *A typeface that is particularly wide or is wider than another typeface in the same family.*

F

F key. *See* PostScript dump

False styles 30–31. *Styles created by the computer algorithmically rather than using the true style, such as italic, bold, or bold italic.*

Family. *See* Fonts. *A set of fonts that share basic characteristics. Most font families include regular (or roman), bold, italic, and bold italic faces. Others include condensed and extended faces.*

Faster bitmap printing. *See* Page Setup

File formats. *See* Graphic file formats

File types 14–19

Film recorders 84, 88, 92

Find/Change 37

First line indent 61–62

Flat bitmapped image 11. *A bitmapped image that only has a pixel depth of one bit. Also called a bilevel or one-bit image.*

Flatness 144. *The amount of calculation that a PostScript interpreter has to do to create a curve. Higher flatness values mean less calculation, faster printing, but rougher curves.*

Flush left. *Aligning text along the left margin. Also called "left aligned" or "ragged right."*

Flush right. *Aligning text along the right margin. Also called "right aligned" or "ragged left."*

Folio. *A page number.*

Font substitution 108–109

Font/DA Mover 26

FontMonger 29, 32

Fontographer 28

Fonts. *See also* False styles
    and System 7 31–34
    copyright issues 34
    Courier 104, 127
    definition 24
    downloading 104–105, 131, 142
    electronic files 25–29
    families 24*
    hinting 27–28*
    loading 26, 127
    monospaced 39, 86*
    on menus 29–31
    printer fonts 27–29, 31–33
    printing 103–105, 114–115, 142
    proportional 39*
    rendering 31–33*
    screen fonts 25–26, 31–33, 163
    sending to service bureau 34, 124, 131
    specimen sheets 163
    suitcases 26, 163*
    transforming 29